BEN SPIES

BEN SPIES

TAKING IT TO THE NEXT LEVEL

LARRY LAWRENCE

FOREWORD BY KEVIN SCHWANTZ

DESIGN BY TOM MORGAN

DAVID BULL PUBLISHING

Library of Congress Control Number: 2011931221

ISBN: 978 1 935007 15 9

David Bull Publishing, logo, and colophon are trademarks of David Bull Publishing, Inc.

Book and cover design: Tom Morgan, Blue Design, Portland, Maine

Printed in China

10 9 8 7 6 5 4 3 2 1

David Bull Publishing
4250 East Camelback Road
Suite K150
Phoenix, AZ 85018

602-852-9500
602-852-9503 (fax)

www.bullpublishing.com

PAGE 2: In 2009, Ben won the World Superbike championship as a rookie. At the U.S. round at Miller Motorsports Park, he dominated the event with a margin of victory in the interrupted first race of 9.394 seconds on aggregate time, and nearly as much in the second—9.080 seconds. (RILES & NELSON)

RIGHT: Lightning strikes in the distance during Saturday practice at Miller Motorsports Park. By winning both races Ben took 35 points out of Nori Haga's championship lead. (ANDREW WHEELER)

PAGE 6: The crowd at a pre-race event at Indianapolis Motor Speedway is reflected in Ben's Oakley sunglasses during a promotional appearance on the first day of the race weekend. Ben would have reason to smile on Sunday when he finished second in the Red Bull Indianapolis Grand Prix riding for Tech 3, Yamaha's satellite MotoGP team. (ANDREW WHEELER)

PAGES 8-9: At Catalunya in 2011, now riding for the Yamaha factory team, Ben demonstrates his characteristically smooth-but-aggressive style and high corner speed. He finished third behind winner Casey Stoner and teammate Jorge Lorenzo. (ANDREW WHEELER)

CONTENTS

The strong relationship between Kevin Schwantz and Ben Spies began in 1999. The two were brought together by a magazine test of various Suzuki GSX-Rs at Oak Hill Raceway in Texas to mark the 15th anniversary of the model. (RILES & NELSON)

FOREWORD

I think I first met Ben at a race when he was 10 or 11 years old, but the first time I really took notice of him was when he was about 15 or so. He was already on John Ulrich's radar when I watched him race a 750 Supersport bike at a WERA event. I knew even then that he had a lot of talent.

I'll never forget the first time I was on the track with Ben. He was still very young, maybe 16 or so. It was at Oak Hill Raceway, and we were doing a special assignment on the anniversary of the Suzuki GSX-R750, going back and comparing GSX-Rs from different eras. He got on this 1986 model with a 2.5-inch rim on the front and a 3.5-inch rim on the rear and he had the thing sideways, smoking the rear tire coming off a corner. I was like, "You've got to be kidding me." Everything he rides is along those same lines. It's, "Let's get the most out of this thing as quickly as I can."

Ben always had the ability to know almost exactly how fast he could ultimately go on the track. That was a skill I never had, and something that really amazed me about Ben. I started working more closely with him when he came to Yoshimura Suzuki. He would come in after a practice and tell me he thought he could shave three-tenths off his lap time. Inevitably he would go out and find that extra three- or four-tenths. When I raced I just went as fast as I could in a given session, and when I came back in I couldn't tell you whether I had even half a tenth left in me. Ben's capacity to be so analytical about his riding was something that impressed me from the start. He could break down and judge parts of the track where he thought he could go faster, or, if he was held up by a slower rider, he knew instinctively what effect that would have on his lap times. He's always been, to say the least, exceptional at that.

In terms of coaching, the one thing I did with Ben that may have been helpful was to teach him to focus on the big picture instead of being so worried about how fast he could go in a single lap. That's something Tom Houseworth and I always tried to emphasize with Ben. An example of Ben's determination to find that perfect lap was in his early years with Yoshimura, when he used more tires than Mat Mladin and Aaron Yates put together. He always wanted to do the fastest lap, but in his first Superbike seasons against Mladin, those fast laps never materialized into a win.

During the winter I encouraged him to train on his motocross bikes or bicycles, where he could turn in his best performance late in the training session. I wanted him to be able to focus on stringing these fast laps together more consistently from start to finish rather than killing it early and having nothing left at the end. I don't think it was ever really his fitness that kept him from being strong at the end of the race; I think it had more to do with his attitude. I was able to convince him that just because he could put new tires on during practice and go out and be faster than Mat, ultimately he needed to ride longer in practice on a race tire and find that consistency in order to put together a complete race.

To his credit, Ben took that advice to heart and really worked on having a little extra. As time went by, Ben learned that if a race came down to the final few laps, he could keep just a little in reserve to call on and close out a race—ultimately, one of his biggest strengths.

This was really the only thing I had to teach Ben. Everything else—his motivation, talent, and focus—all were at a higher level than I had ever reached in my own career. Although I was good at training and putting myself in a position where other riders couldn't see a weakness in me, Ben takes that to a whole new level.

Going back to the American glory years when Wayne Rainey, Eddie Lawson, and I dominated grand prix racing, we were fierce competitors, and each of us was always a threat to win. More than anyone else I've seen since that era, Ben really has that same type of ability to ride around problems and race at the highest level, even when the setup isn't perfect. I know he has the work ethic, and physically and mentally he's as tough as you need to be. Ben's in the right place, he's with a good team, and I think we'll continue to see great things from him.

—KEVIN SCHWANTZ,
1993 GRAND PRIX MOTORCYCLE CHAMPION

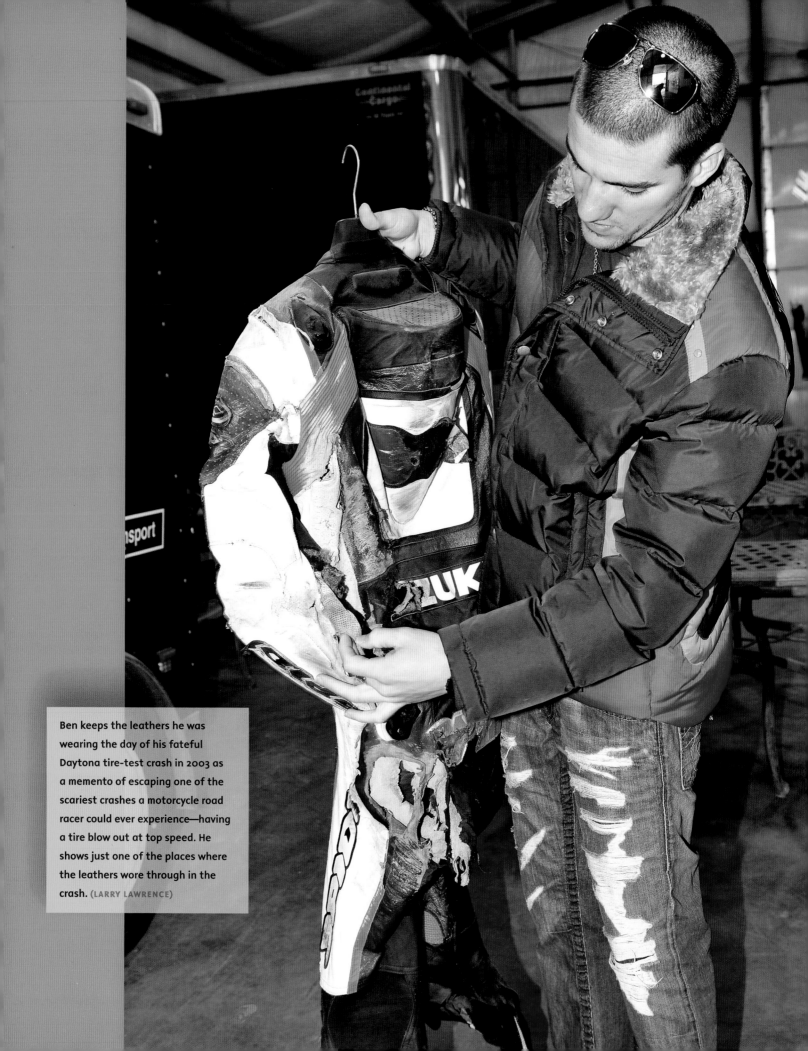

Ben keeps the leathers he was wearing the day of his fateful Daytona tire-test crash in 2003 as a memento of escaping one of the scariest crashes a motorcycle road racer could ever experience—having a tire blow out at top speed. He shows just one of the places where the leathers wore through in the crash. (LARRY LAWRENCE)

CHAPTER 1 — WHAT HAVE I DONE?

en Spies was staring facedown at a cold gray floor. Occasionally he noticed feet and legs, covered in blue medical scrubs, walking in and out of view. Shadows from the bright lighting created a pattern on the floor. It was March 2004, and he was prone on a gurney in Halifax Medical Center, a virtual stone's throw from Daytona International Speedway.

Damn—now I've done it, Ben thought, as nurses put every ounce of strength they had into scrubbing chunks of coal-black pavement out of his raw backside. Even with an IV drip injecting painkiller into his veins, he could still feel them scrubbing and digging. He'd heard that the emergency medical staff at Halifax weren't the biggest fans of motorcycle racers. Riders filled their wards every March, both Daytona racers and the black T-shirt Harley crowd who come down and fill the streets and highways around Daytona Beach during the annual gathering they call Bike Week.

Ben asked a nurse if they were still giving him painkiller, because he was starting to feel things again. He heard mumbling. The nurses had been working so hard on cleaning his wounds that they had forgotten to put more painkiller into his IV. "We'll take care of it," the nurse said.

Select visitors were coming in to see Ben. He couldn't see them, but he could hear his mother's voice among them, talking to the ER staff. She didn't know Ben could hear. He could barely make out what she was saying. "Half of his

ABOVE: **Lisa Spies (Ben's sister) and Ben pose for a family snapshot. Ben says Lisa was primarily responsible for turning him into a daredevil at a young age. Lisa was fully supportive of her brother's racing, and says that despite her family's focus on his career, she never felt deprived in any way. (SPIES COLLECTION)**

butt cheek is gone," Mary cried. Ben wondered what had happened—why he had crashed—and if his racing career might be over.

Daytona International Speedway is a mecca for many disciplines in automotive motorsports, and a living and breathing hell on earth for motorcycle racers. The track—with its steep, high-banked turns, lined with concrete barriers, and its challenging flat infield sections—was never intended for motorcycle racing. Seven-time champion NASCAR driver Dale Earnhardt had died a few years earlier after hitting one of Daytona's unforgiving walls—and he had been protected by the roll cage in a top-team stock car. Imagine what motorcycle racers think of the place.

An hour before his arrival in the ER, Ben had been riding at full speed around Daytona's banking at 186 mph. He was on the last lap of the last day of an exclusive October Dunlop tire test that was a prelude to the more-inclusive December test. He was just about to cross the finish line and blip the throttle for the final time, braking for the first turn, when it happened.

Bam!

What is this? I'm on the ground! he thought. *This can't be.* After he'd fallen, Ben looked over his shoulder and saw the big "I," one of the huge black letters that spells "Daytona International Speedway" in black on the white concrete wall. The back of Ben's head was speeding straight at the big "I" at 260 feet per second, as if it were a giant bull's-eye. Strangely, however, everything seemed to be happening in slow motion.

"I hit the ground fast, but I actually had time to take stock," Ben recalls later. "'Yes, this is really happening; yes, I've been thrown off my motorcycle at top speed; yes, my ass is burning; and yes . . . I'm about to hit the big 'I' with my head.'"

It's amazing how the mind works in these situations. Ben describes it like being in the movie *The Matrix,* where things are happening at hyper speed, but in one's mind's eye, it seems to be moving in super-slow motion. For just a split second, Ben surveyed the scene and was held in suspended wonderment.

"My Suzuki was floating in the air above me like a low-flying, blue-and-white 747," he says. "Pieces of it were slowly being shed. Gas was spewing out, creating a mist that burst through with a rainbow of colors. I slid up the banking. I looked over and saw my right hand; smoke was billowing from underneath my glove. The horizon was tilted at an odd angle. And then I sensed the wall. It was strange because in my mind, there was no sound."

Suddenly, his survival instincts kicked in. Somehow Ben knew exactly what he needed to do. He dug in his left heel for all he was worth, and the added friction swung his body around 180 degrees. He was coming to the wall, but at least he would hit it with his feet and legs, not his head. "My bike hit first right above me," Ben says. "It exploded into a bright-orange ball of flame. I felt intense heat."

Ben made heavy contact with the wall, but it was not as bad as he thought it might be. His last-second sliding maneuver had caused him to strike with a glancing blow. Even though he had glanced off the wall, Ben was not completely spared. The friction of crashing at top speed had abraded his leathers and burned into his skin. "I thought maybe gas had sprayed on me from the bike and I was on fire," he says. "Was I going to survive a 190-mph crash only to be burned alive?"

Even before he came to a complete stop more than 100 yards away from where he had first hit the ground, Ben stood up. "I was done with the ground. My goal was to get up and run to the pit wall so someone could shoot me with a fire extinguisher. I was up running, looking down and behind. Strangely there was no fire, but a smell of something burning. Just then I saw the monstrous gaping hole in the back of my racing leathers."

That wasn't fire Ben smelled; it was leather, and his own tender flesh burning from the friction of that prolonged slide. He looked away, not wanting to see it. He suddenly felt queasy. People were running toward him as he fell to the ground.

Racing leathers have been around for nearly as long as men have been racing motorcycles. Technology has steadily improved, and Ben had crashed dozens of times and had always been able to get up with barely a scratch to show for it. Leathers could easily take a 60-mph crash in a slow

Ben talks with Dunlop's American racing manager Jim Allen (now retired) at Road Atlanta in 2007. Allen said he always appreciated the fact that Ben didn't openly criticize Dunlop after Ben's Daytona tire-test crash. (RILES & NELSON)

turn, or even a 100-mph high-side out of a fast sweeper, but the one thing they weren't designed to handle was sliding on pavement at 186 mph. At that speed, the thick protective layer of cowhide burned through in a fraction of a second, leaving human skin exposed.

Ben had first felt the burning on his backside and arm as he had looked toward the pits, but then he felt okay. Soon afterward, however, his adrenaline started wearing off, and the throbbing pain hit hard, in rapid waves.

"I saw people coming toward me," he says. "I found out later that the team's truck driver, my buddy, Will Bastian, was sitting on the inside wall with the radar gun. The explosion of my bike's rear tire that had caused the whole mess was so loud that Will said he was temporarily deaf in his left ear. While the crew was running toward me,

poor Will was walking away from me with his head down. He just knew I was dead and he couldn't bring himself to look back."

In the group running to Ben's assistance was Mary, his mother. She ran harder than any woman in heels should be able to run. One of her shoes went flying and then her asthma kicked in, but she never broke stride. Passing her was Ben's mechanic, Tom Houseworth. He was at full throttle on a quad and would have broken down a brick wall to reach Ben. Also going at a quick clip was Yoshimura Suzuki team manager Don Sakakura, who had seen too many accidents like Ben's and had a grim sense of foreboding.

Ben was in severe pain by the time help reached him. The burning was unbearable. He clenched his teeth and asked Tom how bad it was, but when their eyes met, Tom didn't

In 2004 Ben came back from his Daytona tire-test crash and won three nationals—two in Superstock and one in Supersport—despite the fact that he was still recovering from his injuries for much of the season. This is Ben racing his Suzuki GSX-R600 Supersport machine. He won the Supersport race at Infineon on this bike, even though it was considered underpowered. (RILES & NELSON)

Ben talks with his crew chief Tom Houseworth at Fontana in 2004. Houseworth, or "House," as his friends call him, has worked with Ben since November of 2002 when Ben signed with Yoshimura Suzuki. The duo has become one of the most successful rider / crew chief combinations in motorcycle roadracing. (RILES & NELSON)

have to say a word. Ben knew by the look on his face. The ambulance pulled up, and the paramedics leapt out and started evaluating Ben's injuries. His leathers were still hot and he screamed for them to be cut off. They stood frozen at the request. "In retrospect, I'm sure they were trying to figure out the best course of action, but my mom heard me say I wanted my leathers off, and that was her cue to begin ripping into them."

"Don't do that—he might have a broken back," one of the paramedics cautioned. "Wait until we find our scissors."

"Don't just stand there! Find those damn scissors now!" Mary screamed.

The leathers were cut off, and Ben was carried into the ambulance. They rushed through Daytona's infield, the paramedics talking about taking him to the infield care center. Mary and Tom both yelled for them to take Ben directly to the hospital. Tom told them to stop as they came up to Ben's motor coach. Houseworth jumped out, ran and grabbed some shoes, and handed them to Mary. With that the doors were closed. It was eerily quiet, with only the humming sound of medical equipment. It was just Ben, Mary, and the paramedics rolling toward Halifax. Every tiny bump on the short drive was magnified to an alarming degree and shot waves of pain up Ben's spine. In a few minutes, he would reach Halifax Medical Center, and a new kind of pain would begin.

Ben's harrowing Daytona crash happened when he was just 19. It was a pivotal time in his life: He was still young enough that he could have easily considered other options to pursue in his future. Many members of his family were just getting used to the fact that racing was what Ben would be doing for a living, and now this—a crash that could have turned out much worse than it did. But in Ben's mind, the crash was never going to alter his goals.

"Getting injured is part of the price you pay sometimes to be a professional motorcycle racer," Ben says. "Obviously, you don't expect to have a tire blow while you're running at top speed, but you know crashes are going to happen. I never had any doubts about coming back to racing. I was

asking the doctors from the start when I could get back on the bike, when I could start training again."

But while the Daytona crash didn't deter Ben, Mary says it made the family reconsider his course. "I was horrified by Ben's crash and his injuries," Mary remembers. "There were a lot of discussions within the family about whether this might be the time for Ben to seriously consider if this was really what he wanted to do with his life. Henry was concerned, as any father would be, and I had my doubts, no question. You can't see your son go through something like that and not wonder if we'd helped him down the wrong path, but there was never any question with him."

The crash also revealed the depth of Ben's character to some inside the industry. Jim Allen, who was heading up Dunlop's racing program at the time, later said he admired how Ben had handled the aftermath of the Daytona crash.

"Ben could have been very critical publicly about what happened at Daytona, and no one would have blamed him," Allen says. "But he kept his discussions with Dunlop between us, and his public stance was one where he said he understood that the company was doing all it could to solve the problem we were having in developing a tire that would endure those kinds of stresses. That was really something for a kid of his age to show that kind of understanding."

The Daytona incident and the way Ben rose to meet the challenges are emblematic of the way he would face many obstacles in his career. His mental toughness, his focus, his understanding of risks and his own limits, and his ability to overcome injuries are among the characteristics that would elevate Ben from being a talented club racer to becoming one of the world's elite motorcycle road racers.

Showing his Texas roots, toddler Ben sports a pair of overalls. Mary remembers Ben as a happy baby, always smiling, laughing, and playing. (SPIES COLLECTION)

CHAPTER 2 — A LIONESS MOTHER

s a consequence of the horrific crash at Daytona, Ben would have to endure painful skin grafts and a prolonged period of healing, followed by rehabilitation to get his full range of motion back. He hardly considered that he would be permanently scarred, looking instead at his etched skin as a constant reminder of the price he had paid to reach his goal of becoming a professional racer. Even at the age of 19, Ben had developed an attitude of gritty determination. He looked beyond immediate problems and sought solutions that would help him continue to strive toward his goals.

To understand where much of Ben's resolute determination comes from, one need look no further than his mother. Mary Spies, perhaps more than any other mother in the paddock, has been side by side and involved in her son's racing career from day one. It was Mary who found ways for Ben to have more time to practice than his competitors. It was Mary who shepherded her son from the amateur ranks to a path that would lead him to become a professional. Acting as manager, scheduler, equipment manager, and primary cheerleader, she has been described as a lioness forcefully protecting her cub. Some say she's overly aggressive, too blunt, and meddlesome.

ABOVE: **Baby Ben wearing a monogrammed jumpsuit in a baby portrait. With a loving mother and doting sister, he was undoubtedly the center of attention in the Spies household. (SPIES COLLECTION)**

It's not like Mary isn't aware of the kind of talk she generates. "I know some people think I'm the ultimate stage mom," Mary famously said in an interview early in Ben's career, "but people tend to forget that Ben was a child when he turned pro. I really won't take no for an answer when I want something for my son that I think is the best for him. I'm his mother, and knowing him his whole life and all the dreams that he's had, his goals, and what he's done, and what he's given up to do this, he deserves what he asks for."

Mary grew up in Dallas, the daughter of Bill Barrett, one of the biggest beer distributors in America. "Schlitz put me through diapers, Lone Star put me through elementary, and Coors put me through high school and college," Mary says with a laugh. The middle of five children with an older brother and sister and a younger brother and sister, Mary lived a comfortable life, attended Catholic schools, and did most of what upper-middle-class Baby Boomer–generation girls from Texas did. She played the piano, tap-danced, roller-skated, and sang in the choir. Mary had a down-home streak in her, as well. One of her favorite pastimes was fishing, using crawdads as bait.

Perhaps her most vivid memory as a young girl was the assassination of President John F. Kennedy. It was especially tough on those who lived in Dallas, because the assassination took place in their hometown. Mary remembers one of her fellow students' mothers coming into her class, sobbing uncontrollably and telling the class that President Kennedy had been shot. "We were all in a daze," Mary remembers of the November 22, 1963, assassination. "Everyone loved President Kennedy, especially, as you might imagine, at a Catholic school."

Mary's mother and grandmother were very strong and independent women, especially for their time. Mary absorbed that influence, and she credits them for the mental toughness and focused determination she exhibited as an adult.

"I believe the Irish nuns had an influence that also made me very independent and confident," Mary explains. "The hardness I sometimes have is something that was only acquired after dealing with men in the motorcycle industry who just weren't used to dealing with a woman on a business level. It was hard at times for my siblings and friends to watch the change or see the armor come up."

Mary went to college at Stephen F. Austin State University in Nacogdoches, Texas, and that's where she met Ben's father, Henry Spies. "I was yelling out from a third-story window in my dorm to a friend, and Henry, who was cutting grass, found a way to get into the conversation," Mary says of their first meeting.

Henry had grown up in Nacogdoches, and was a fellow student at the university. The two soon began dating, and a little over two years after they first met, Mary and Henry married, in 1973. Henry's father had ridden motorcycles as a young man, but had given up the sport early on. Henry himself was more into hot rods and fast cars.

Henry took a job right out of college with a company that was a division of metals manufacturing giant Alcoa. He would eventually become an executive with the company. (After it was bought and sold several times, Henry would take an early-retirement offer after 31 years with the company.) The couple had settled in Longview, Texas, where Henry was working, and they looked destined to have a normal suburban American existence.

They wanted to start a family, but after trying for five years, Mary could not become pregnant. Mary says the doctors could never give her a definitive reason for her inability to conceive, although one speculated that she suffered from Stein-Leventhal syndrome, a disorder characterized by infrequent or absent ovulation. In 1980 they decided to adopt and were blessed with baby Lisa.

Lisa was a beautiful child, with Shirley Temple curls and chubby little arms, and she brought much joy to the Spies household. One day when Lisa was three she came into the kitchen while Mary was making spaghetti and asked her mom for a baby brother. "Mommy's tummy is broken, remember?" Mary said to her little girl. "You came from Mommy's heart."

Little Lisa put her hands on her hips and bounced her little curls, saying, "God loves me, and if I want a baby brother, he's going to give me a baby brother!" And with that she stomped out of the kitchen.

A few weeks later Mary started having morning sickness. The family was readying to move to Memphis, the result of a job transfer for Henry. Initially her doctor told her the morn-

ing sickness was probably an ulcer from the stress of getting ready to move. But she kept getting sicker, and finally another doctor told her it sounded like she was pregnant.

"I told them it was not possible," Mary remembers. "But they did tests, and sure enough, I was pregnant. I learned two things that day: One was that Ben was a blessed surprise, and two, that you don't mess around with Lisa. When she wants something she's going to get it."

Shortly thereafter, the Spies family moved to the Memphis suburb of Germantown, Tennessee, and Ben was born in Memphis, at Baptist Memorial Hospital, on July 11, 1984. He was 7 pounds, 6 ounces, and 20 inches long.

When Ben was only eight months old, the family returned to Longview, Texas—the place Ben has always considered his hometown—the result of another promotion and job relocation for Henry.

It didn't take long for the Spies family to recognize that Ben most definitely had a daredevil streak in him. Here he performs on one of his first bicycles. (SPIES COLLECTION)

CHAPTER 3 — LONGVIEW, TEXAS

Longview is a town of about 80,000 in East Texas. Its slightly rolling terrain covered by tall pines makes it look more like northern Georgia than the typical image of Texas. Even though it was a pretty good-sized town, Ben grew up feeling that he knew practically everybody in his neighborhood, and that everybody knew him.

"Longview had a small-town feel," Ben says. "All the neighborhood kids knew who gave out the good candy at Halloween and stuff like that. There was one house down the street that was set back in a heavily wooded lot and sort of spooky, and the people who lived there were real private. So we had our own little neighborhood haunted house. It was a fun place to grow up as a kid. We always had things to do."

Having grown up in Dallas, Mary considered Longview a little sleepy, but she agrees that it was a nice town in which to raise a family. "It was a place where everyone looked out for each other's kids," Mary says. "I was never worried about letting Lisa and Ben go out and play. It was safe and cozy."

As a toddler Ben demonstrated a great sense of humor. His sister Lisa always had fun dressing him up in crazy outfits, and Ben happily went along with it, knowing he was going to make his family and friends laugh.

Whereas many sisters like to shelter and protect their baby brothers, Lisa was the opposite. She encouraged her little brother's daredevil tendencies. When Longview got one of its infrequent snows during the winter, it was Lisa who pushed Ben down the steepest hill on a greased cookie sheet. "One day I looked out the window and Ben and Lisa were sliding down this hill right into the street," Mary remembers. "They

ABOVE: A dapper Ben dressed up in a suit for a portrait taken when he was nine years old.
(SPIES COLLECTION)

were laughing and having a good old time, oblivious to any cars that might have been coming down the road."

Lisa recalls other childhood examples of egging her brother on to perform daredevil feats. "There were woods across the street from our house. The trees had big vines hanging down, and Ben and I would go over and play Tarzan on them. He went from that to jumping from the roof of our house to our neighbors' roof, the whole time knowing that if he got hurt, I'd be the one in trouble because I was supposed to be watching him."

Ben and Lisa shared a little battery-powered go-kart that they would ride to the top of a steep neighborhood hill; once there, they would cut the power and coast it down the hill as fast as it would go. "The only way we could really stop the thing was to run it into a curb and hope that it didn't hop over and crash into a tree or mailbox," Lisa says. Despite the risky nature of their stunts, these outings seldom ended in tears.

"A lot of sisters either ignore their little brother or try to baby them," Ben says. "Lisa wasn't like that. We were always doing crazy stuff on bicycles, little go-karts, or things like that. When I wanted to jump over a curb, build a ramp, ride down a super-steep hill or something, she actually encouraged me. Looking back, I don't know if she wanted to see me get hurt or what. She really did look after me. I think she somehow knew I would take things to the edge

of being out of control, but I had just enough of a self-preservation instinct to not go over that edge."

Once he started school Ben's biggest joy was playing sports. He started with grade-school kickball, often played on the paved playgrounds. "Ben just loved kicking that ball, and he could really boot it," Mary recalls. "But when he played he really didn't care much about the rules of the game. Kicking the ball as far as he could—that's all he cared about. We had to yell and encourage him to run to first base because sometimes he'd get so excited about his kick that he'd take off for third base."

As he got older it became obvious that Ben was a natural athlete. He excelled at every sport he tried. Lisa tells the story of dropping him off to play pickup football with a group of neighborhood boys. "He'd never played before," Lisa says, "but by the time I came back to pick him up, he was playing quarterback and calling all the plays. He was just a natural leader and picked up things very quickly."

Although Ben played football and basketball, he really excelled in baseball as a pitcher. He was a lefty, which gave him a natural advantage against batters who mostly faced right-handed pitchers. He also developed a mean breaking ball that would drop off the shelf just before it crossed the plate. Ben's uncle John was a semipro baseball player, and he marveled at young Ben's pitching ability.

"I just know that if he hadn't gotten into motorcycles, he would have had a future in baseball," Mary says. "He was a naturally talented pitcher, and in Little League batters just had a tough time hitting off of him."

Riding his bicycle was another favorite activity for Ben. When he was just three he surprised his dad. "We had moved to a new house and the movers had broken or bent one of the training wheels on Ben's bicycle," Henry says. "He asked

LEFT: Instead of coddling her baby brother, Lisa encouraged Ben to be daring from a young age. She was a bit of a speed demon herself. Here she is, driving a go-kart down their neighborhood street. (SPIES COLLECTION)

BELOW LEFT: Ben excelled at many different sports as a kid, but showed particular promise as a pitcher in youth baseball. Despite being relatively small for his age, he was always one of the top pitchers in Little League. (SPIES COLLECTION)

BELOW CENTER: Ben wearing one of his favorite T-shirts as a young boy. Lisa says she and her friends liked to dress Ben up in all kinds of crazy outfits when he was little. Ben was game, and always tried to make his friends and family laugh with the funny outfits he wore. (SPIES COLLECTION)

BELOW RIGHT: Soccer was another sport Ben played as a youth. Here he poses for a photo while playing youth soccer in Rockwall County, Texas. (SPIES COLLECTION)

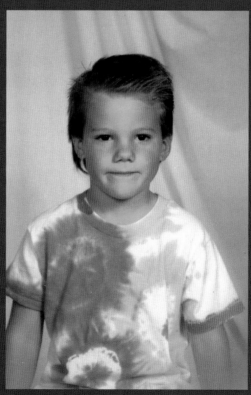

LEFT: It was normal for kids growing up in East Texas to take up hunting at a young age, and Ben was no different. Here he shows off his quarry of wild turkey. (SPIES COLLECTION) BELOW: Ben and Lisa taking it easy in a hammock on a lazy summer afternoon. The two went through a lot together as children and remain very close as adults today. (SPIES COLLECTION)

me to fix it as I was walking out the door. I told him I would fix it as soon as I got home. When I got back that night he had somehow managed to take off the other training wheel and was riding the bicycle without them."

Ben was a terror on his bicycle. Family photos show Ben at four or five riding his bicycle while standing up, one foot on the seat, the other on the top tube of the frame. He was a fearless kid, and a quick learner. He rarely seemed to pay the price for his high-risk antics. While his stunts looked too advanced for a child his age, his sister claims he always had some innate ability to take things right to the edge without going past the point of no return.

While Ben's early childhood seems idyllic, it turns out that not everything was rosy. There were problems in Mary and Henry's marriage. Even though Mary and Henry were devoted to their children, they found themselves drifting apart as a couple.

"We had completely opposite ideas of how to raise Ben and Lisa," Mary says. "Henry was probably more a typical parent, and I was definitely unconventional, I would say. I wanted to let the kids do what they wanted to do. I felt that was the best way for them to grow, explore, and find out what their interests would be. It was difficult for Henry to accept this open approach to parenting, and eventually it became an obstacle between us that we couldn't overcome."

Ben was just four when his parents split. "He cried almost every night for a year," Mary says of Ben, after his dad no longer lived in the family home. "He was too little to understand. He just knew his daddy wasn't there."

While the split-up and eventual divorce of his parents was indeed painful for Ben, he was fortunate to have an extended family, with grandparents, aunts, and uncles. As a result, he always had a deep sense of family. Also, both of his parents recognized the importance of keeping Henry in Ben's life. While Ben spent the vast majority of his childhood living with his mother, Henry remained in his children's lives and shared custody of Lisa and Ben.

Fortunately for young Ben, a new passion was soon to enter his life that would take the focus off his parents' divorce. Ben's fascination with motorcycles started at an early age. A neighbor kept a street bike in his garage, and whenever Ben came over to that neighbor's house all he wanted to do was touch the bike and stare at it. "From the time he saw our neighbor's motorcycle when he was about four or five, he noticed motorcycles wherever we went," Mary says. "If we were in the car and a motorcycle would pull up, he would just push his face close to the window and watch very intently."

His enthrallment with bikes got even more intense when Mary and Henry took Ben to Texas Stadium, in the Dallas suburb of Irving, Texas, to watch his first motorcycle race, an AMA Supercross event. "After that, dirt bikes were all he talked about," Mary remembers.

Although Ben was fascinated by motorcycles, he was too young to have one. His father wasn't interested in motorcycles at all, and his mother didn't know enough about them to even consider buying him one. For the moment, riding his bicycle and imagining it was a motorcycle was as close as Ben was going to get to the real thing.

Ben's growing obsession with motorcycles made it tough to get him to focus on anything else. Mary remembers that a few years later, when he was in grade school, his teachers would call her, somewhat concerned. "Ben only wanted to read books that had to do with motorcycles," Mary says, remembering the teachers' worry. "Any written story assignment he turned in had something to do with motorcycles. They wanted him to write something for once that didn't have to do with motorcycles, but he wouldn't do it."

A new person was about to come into Mary, Ben, and Lisa's life. This person's influence would ultimately be most profound for Ben, who would finally gain access to the thing he craved most.

Many road racers like the Hayden brothers got started by racing flat-track. While Ben never formally raced flat-track events, he spent days on end running laps on a short track he and Keith Cherry had laid out on oil-drilling land owned by Cherry's family. (SPIES COLLECTION)

CHAPTER 4 — A MOTORCYCLE MENTOR

I t's hard to imagine that a racquetball lesson would lead to Ben Spies becoming a motorcycle road racer, but that's exactly what happened. Although Keith Cherry worked in his family's oil company, he had been a professional racquetball player and was a part-time instructor at the local club. Mary signed Lisa up for lessons with Cherry. Ben would watch intently as Keith worked with his sister, and the two quickly became buddies when Ben was barely five.

The interest the Spies children showed in Keith was soon shared by their mother. A lunch date led to dinner, and gradually Keith and Mary began a relationship that would last for nearly 10 years.

Cherry first helped Ben in sports, coaching him in Little League baseball and practicing basketball. But for Cherry these training sessions were more than just casual play. He felt he should toughen Ben up by not letting him win, pushing him to work hard if he wanted to make a basket or hit a baseball. Keith's "tough love" approach to coaching Ben in athletics would be applied again later when he got Ben into motorcycle racing.

When Keith was growing up, his East Texas oilman father didn't want to make the path easy for his son. "That's just the way a lot of fathers were then, and maybe still are," Keith says. "They wanted you to find your own way, show some initiative. Nothing was going to be handed to me on a silver platter."

ABOVE: Ben's little Yamaha PW50, a shaft-driven, two-stroke mini dirt bike, has long been a staple for youth riders. Ben spent hours riding this little motorcycle around a nearby field and also created a little track in his front yard. (SPIES COLLECTION)

Instead of taking a position with his father's company right out of college, Keith struck out on his own, trying to find work in the then-depressed oil business, doing other jobs before ultimately going back to continue his education. Teaching boys to become independent, strong, and self-sufficient men is deeply rooted in Texas culture, and since Keith was raised without much praise, and without any shielding, that's the way he approached what would become his father-like relationship with Ben.

Keith had been a casual motorcyclist, but after moving back to his hometown of Longview from Houston, he met some friends who road-raced motorcycles. He started going to the races himself, gradually growing more interested in the sport. During one race weekend at Oak Hill Raceway, Keith met the Hayden family. Keith took the Haydens to a buddy's Baskin-Robbins store to treat them to ice cream after the race and became friends with Earl Hayden, the father of rac-

ers Nicky, Tommy, and Roger. Keith later bought used Yamaha YSR50 race bikes from Earl and began racing them himself.

"I remember Keith taking us to the ice cream shop," Earl Hayden says. "He was a real nice guy, and wanted to learn everything he could about racing. I never realized it until years later that some of the first race bikes Ben ever raced were once my boys' bikes. It's funny how the motorcycle racing community is so close and tightly knit. You hear stories like that all the time, and I think it's great that we have a connection like that to Ben."

Ben's own dream of having a motorcycle came true one day when Keith brought him a Yamaha PW50. "I remember

I just drove up out of the clear blue with this bike," Keith says. "I think Mary was a little irritated with me because I hadn't discussed it with her beforehand. She was also maybe a little scared. She'd never been around motorcycles and didn't know anything about them."

To Mary's relief the bike was just a tad too big for Ben—plus, he was still scared of the noise it made. He would cover his ears when it was started. Nevertheless, it didn't take him long to get used to the bike. Training wheels took care of the problem of the mini-bike being too tall, and wearing a helmet cut down on the noise Ben had to endure. Within two weeks Ben had mastered the PW50 and was ready to ride it beyond his yard and driveway.

"I was probably only five or six, so I don't remember too much about that first bike, other than I do remember covering my ears," Ben says. "I loved motorcycles, but for some reason, the noise scared me."

Keith had a motocross bike, and the two rode for hours on a little dirt track near Ben's house. It wasn't long before the training wheels came off and Ben really started learning how to ride.

"We would ride on oil-lease land. There were little flags set up to mark where pipelines were laid," Keith explains. "We would just race from flag to flag and make a little flat-track course."

From the beginning, riding for Ben quickly turned into racing sessions against the clock, or against Keith. His daredevil, competitive spirit was piqued. All those times when Lisa had pushed her little brother to try to jump farther or ride faster on his bicycle or go-kart were now a major influence on how Ben learned to ride a motorcycle. He instinctively pushed himself to ride the little mini-bike to the limits of his abilities. Even though he was being pushed to ride faster, Ben loved every minute of it. He got almost as much enjoyment when he was given his first set of motocross gear as he did from the little mini-bike.

"There wasn't any playing around," Keith says. "I always told him to ride with a purpose. Before I knew it he was nipping at my heels, even though I had a bigger bike. He was a fast learner on the bike even from the start."

When the AMA Superbike Championship came to the Texas World Speedway in 1992, Keith and Mary rented a motor home and took Ben to his first pro Superbike race. Ben had pictures taken standing with Scott Russell, a factory Kawasaki rider who was his big hero at the time. "I liked Scott [Russell] because he was 'The Chief' and wore that helmet with the Indian headdress painted on it," Ben recalls. For Ben, an aspiring racer, this persona was the coolest thing he could imagine.

The AMA Superbike races at Texas World clearly made a lasting impression on eight-year-old Ben. He watched roadracing any time it was on, read all the motorcycle magazines, and memorized the names and bikes of all the top AMA Superbike and grand prix riders. "Those were the days of Scott Russell, Jamie James, Thomas Stevens, Doug Polen, Tom Kipp, and guys like that," Ben says. "Freddie Spencer was on those red, white, and blue Two Brothers

TOP: Ben and Mary take in their first professional AMA road race as spectators. Mary was a big fan of some of the riders and poses here with AMA and World Superbike Champion Fred Merkel at Texas World Speedway in the early 1990s. (SPIES COLLECTION) BOTTOM: Ben was given a Honda dirt bike for Christmas. It was too cold and snowy outside, so some plywood was laid down for Ben to ride the motorcycle a few laps through the house. (SPIES COLLECTION)

Hondas. I thought that was the coolest-looking motorcycle out there."

Keith clearly remembers Ben having an amazing ability to concentrate when racing. "Most eight-year-olds don't have the attention span to watch an hour-long road-racing program on TV," he says, "but Ben would sit there and watch the entire show intently. Later, after Ben started racing, we would watch racing tapes over and over again, and he would study what the riders were doing on their bikes."

Soon Ben advanced from the PW50 to an 80cc bike with a clutch, followed by a 100cc Honda, and that's about the time he started being able to hang with Keith on his 250cc dirt bike. By then, it was obvious Ben was destined for the race track, but he was already tiring of his dirt bikes. Motocross wasn't in Ben's future. Even as an eight-year-old he knew roadracing was what he wanted to do.

Ben got one of his bikes as a Christmas present. There was snow on the ground outside, so they got some plywood, laid it out on the floor, and let Ben ride the bike around inside the house. "That lasted until the smoke started filling up the place," Mary recalls. "We were lucky we didn't pass out from the fumes."

On the advice of Earl Hayden, Keith took Ben out to a parking lot for his first rides on the YSR50 road-race machines. "I always thought it was important to let the kids ride the bikes and get used to them, get the feel for them before putting them on the track to race," Earl says.

"In the parking lot of Doris McQueen Elementary I set up some orange cones and took him out to ride on the pavement for the first time," Keith recalls. "The one thing he really wanted to do was to drag his knee. He tried and tried, but didn't do it that first time out."

As Ben got more confident on the YSR he came closer and closer to his goal of touching his knee down. He remembers the first time it happened. "I kept putting my knee out to touch, and the first time it did, it scared me so much I nearly fell off the bike."

"People ask me all the time how I got the ability to qualify so well, and I think it all goes back to those days with me on a mini-bike in a parking lot or on the track, with Keith or my mom clocking every lap."

Ben spent hours riding his dirt bikes on land owned by Keith Cherry, who laid out several types of tracks for Ben to practice on. Cherry was quite regimented in supervising Ben's practices, clocking nearly every lap. The goal was to always better the time he had set in the last session.

(SPIES COLLECTION)

When Ben was unable to get to the track to practice, he would often run laps around the driveway of the family home in Longview. (SPIES COLLECTION)

In spite of having a relatively small yard at their Longview home, Ben fashioned a tight little motocross course where he would practice for hours. (SPIES COLLECTION)

Oak Hill Raceway is a serpentine little 1.8-mile, 13-turn road course built in the mid-1970s by a couple of go-kart racing brothers, Jack and Pete Reed. The track proved to be a great training ground for many riders who cut their teeth racing on the challenging course just outside Oak Hill, Texas. Fortunately for Ben, he only lived a half-hour from the track, which could be rented for $100 per day.

With Ben showing as much promise on the pavement as he did on dirt, Keith went into full training mode. "I'd go out and rent the track in the middle of the week, and no one else would be there," Keith recalls. "We started pulling Ben out of school as often as once a week, and putting him on one of the YSR50s. Even though he was underage to be riding on the track, there was no one there to say anything."

With Oak Hill serving as a playground and a get-out-of-school-free card, the days spent at the track became Ben's favorite activity. Soon the dirt bikes were gathering dust, and Ben was focused on being a road racer.

Mary started getting too many questions about Ben's regular absences from the public school he attended, so she pulled him out and enrolled him in an expensive private school where she sometimes worked as a substitute teacher.

"Even though Ben missed some school, we made sure he always did his work and kept his grades up," Mary says in defense of pulling her third-grader out of school to practice roadracing. "I know I raised Ben a little unconventionally, and I make no apologies for that. Especially as he got older, it was obvious that he had a special talent, and racing was what he wanted to do. I always wanted to raise Ben and Lisa with the freedom that most people might find a little odd, but they were always involved in activities and occupied their time with constructive things they enjoyed.

"Whatever my children wanted to do, I was going to go through hell or high water to make it happen. So many of the kids that grew up with Ben in school are into drugs or alcohol, so I really think I made the right decision."

And under Keith's watchful eye the practice sessions in school parking lots and at Oak Hill Raceway were not just playtime for Ben. Keith pushed him to improve his riding, to better his lap times on the little Yamahas. Unlike most motorcycle racers who learn by playing on their motorcycles in the early years, by comparison, Ben's time on motorcycles was regimented almost from the start. Far from resenting it, Ben seemed to thrive at meeting and exceeding the goals he was given. He loved to continually break his own lap record in these weekly sessions.

Many years later, when Ben was breaking lap records at almost every track in World Superbike, people seemed amazed at his ability to quickly learn tracks he'd never raced—and not just learn them but set poles and lap records first time out. Having raced the clock since he was eight, Ben himself doesn't know exactly where the ability to go fast on a new track comes from, but it seems natural to him and is definitely something ingrained in him from doing it nearly his entire life.

"I know I used to bug people all the time when I first started racing, about finding out what their lap times were," Ben recalls. "It was sort of the running joke when they saw me walking down pit lane toward their pits. 'Here comes little Ben again to find out what my lap time was.' You know, people can say this or that about how they're riding or about how fast their bike is, but the stopwatch doesn't lie. It's right there telling you if you're doing better or if the setup changes worked. I think as a kid I wanted to cut through all the bull and get straight to what mattered, and lap times were really it for me.

"People ask me all the time how I got the ability to qualify so well, and I think it all goes back to those days with me on a mini-bike in a parking lot or on the track, with Keith or my mom clocking every lap."

Ben racing on his first road race bike, a 50cc Yamaha. This bike was recently found, restored and presented to Ben as a Christmas present. (SPIES COLLECTION)

CHAPTER 5 – PAVEMENT PRIMARY SCHOOL

en and Keith Cherry first got into roadracing through some friends who were members of the Central Motorcycle Roadracing Association (CMRA). This club-racing organization was founded in 1974 by a University of Texas law student and racer named Lou Linden. For 35 years, the CMRA has held races in Texas and Oklahoma at tracks like Oak Hill Raceway, Texas World Speedway, Hallett Motor Speedway, and other circuits over the years, including street courses. The club has been the launching pad for many of America's top road racers, an inordinate number of whom went on to win World Championships. The roster of former CMRA racers reads like a who's who of American motorcycle roadracing: World Champions Freddie Spencer, Kevin Schwantz, Doug Polen, John Kocinski, Nicky Hayden, and Colin Edwards, as well as a host of top national racers.

ABOVE: Nine years old and ready to take on the world. The Texas club-racing organization bent the rules to allow Ben to race a year before most kids because of the hours of roadracing practice he had already accumulated at Oak Hill Raceway. **(SPIES COLLECTION)**

Keith knew Ben was fast enough to race and be competitive in the CMRA 50cc races. Ben was campaigning the ex-Hayden YSR50s and was getting hours of track time every week at Oak Hill. There was only one problem: The club didn't allow kids to start racing until they were 10, and Ben was just 8.

"I talked to Connie Brothers, who was running the races at the time, and convinced her to let Ben give it a try," Keith recalls. "I knew how good he was, and they had these rider schools, and I said all I wanted was for him to get in the school on the YSR50 and have the instructors watch him and see if they thought he was ready to race."

Brothers was reluctant, but went ahead and allowed Ben to enter riders' school. It turned out to be an easy decision for the instructors when they saw how talented this little eight-year-old rider was in the school. How could they have known about all the seat time at Oak Hill that Ben already had under his belt?

"The instructors couldn't believe how good he was," Keith says. "Even though he was officially too young, they made an exception and went ahead and gave the approval to allow Ben to race."

That was how Keith remembered it, but Mary says the actual story was that Keith lied about Ben's age in order to get him started in the club, and when Connie Brothers found out she was furious. Eventually things were smoothed over and Ben was permitted to continue racing.

"The funny thing was, the CMRA had a written exam that rider-school students had to pass," Mary says with a smile. "Ben was so young he didn't understand all the questions, so Connie's husband read some of the tougher questions to Ben so he could get through it. The wonderful part was that he didn't miss one answer."

In preparation for roadracing Keith and Mary went out and ordered Ben's first set of roadracing gear—blue-and-white Nankai leathers with matching boots and a Bieffe helmet. He was now properly equipped to be a road racer.

The first race Ben entered was at Oak Hill. He lasted three turns. "I crashed," Ben says with a grin. "I started on the last row and was already up to about third when I ran into the back of a guy and went down. Someone has a tape of it somewhere and must be laughing their butt off at it now. I was crying and it wasn't because I'd crashed. I was crying because rider-school students have to wear a yellow T-shirt over their leathers, and if you crashed in your first race you had to wear that T-shirt again in your next three races, and I was pretty upset about that."

Mary remembers the crash and was scared to death because Ben just laid there for the longest time without moving. "Someone had told him not to move after he crashed," she says. "He wasn't hurt at all, but he just laid there like he was told."

In spite of the tough start to his racing career, it wasn't long before the little underage racer started winning. "He was fast right off the bat," Keith says. "He was the fastest kid out there on the 50s, and only a few adults could beat him. It wasn't long before he beat them too."

Ben was a gifted rider, and he had the advantage of the weekly all-day riding session at Oak Hill. Where most kids his age were spending time in a batting cage, learning to hit a baseball, or in soccer practice shooting goals, Ben was practicing hitting his apexes and brake markers and dragging his knee through turns at 80 miles per hour.

Racing became a blur for the nine-year-old kid, to the extent that Ben doesn't remember his first victory. "We raced with the experts and novices on the track at the same time, so the first race I won as a novice I wasn't the first finisher," he explains. "Plus, I was so young and raced so much, a lot of those early years sort of run together. I just know I had a lot of trophies."

Ben was becoming a favorite of fellow CMRA club members and racers. He was a cute little kid who happened to be fast. He always took an interest in what other riders were doing, hung out with them between races, and made friends quickly. He was polite and not too cocky about his abilities. The older riders could already sense that their little buddy had some real potential. They'd seen what the Hayden boys had done a few years earlier, and now it looked like they had a homegrown talent of equal caliber on their hands. Texas riders take pride in helping to produce great racers.

Ben gets ready to compete in his first official road race. "The thing I hated most was wearing the T-shirt they made first-time riders wear," Ben recalls. He cried when he crashed during his first race—not because he was hurt but because he would have to wear the rookie T-shirt for one more race weekend. (SPIES COLLECTION)

Keith Cherry and Ben relax in the paddock before a race. Cherry was Mary's boyfriend and a father figure to Ben, and responsible for getting Ben into racing. A club racer himself, Cherry tried to coach Ben the best he could, but his lack of racing knowledge sometimes got Ben into trouble. (SPIES COLLECTION)

These photos (above, below and opposite) show Ben racing in 1995 on Yamaha YZR50s. He often raced against adults, so it was a treat when the Hayden boys would sometimes come from Kentucky to race in Texas. Ben was closest in age to Roger Lee Hayden, and the two often raced one another as they came up through the club ranks. (SPIES COLLECTION)

As he'd done on dirt bikes, Ben was quickly progressing on roadracing machines, as well. Over the course of a couple of seasons he went from the beginner Yamaha YSR50 to the same bike with an 80cc engine. It was a dream setup. Keith was racing too, and they formed a team called Keith Cherry Racing. The crew started traveling the CMRA circuit with a truck, pulling a trailer full of motorcycles.

On their first visit to Hallett Raceway in Oklahoma, the Cherry/Spies clan had a little dustup with the kings of that track, the McDonalds. Keith, Ben, and Mary had arrived early on a Thursday night to prepare for that weekend's races. They were the first ones at the track, so they set up their gear in one of the few covered garages, thinking it was first come, first served. The next morning Sam McDonald, an ex-factory AMA Superbike rider who, along with his brother Phil, had dominated Hallett for years, showed up, and in no uncertain terms let Keith know that the garage was meant for him, and that they would have to vacate immediately.

"Now, you can imagine that didn't go over with me, and you know it didn't sit well with Mary," Keith says with a laugh. "We had quite a little discussion, and since they ran the races, they won. We went and had to sit out in the sun. Later we found the McDonalds were great people, but I won't lie, I never was a big fan of Sam's, and I loved it when a few years later Ben came up there with a 250 and kicked Sam's butt on his own track."

There were more controversies following Ben in his early racing days. One particular incident rattled Mary. Despite the fact that she was constantly concerned about her son's safety, the wife of another rider threatened to report Mary to child protective services for allowing Ben to race at such a young age.

"This was a lady whose husband was getting beat by Ben," Mary explains. "She came up to me when we were registering for a race and said, 'You shouldn't allow your son to race. He's not old enough to make a decision to do something that is so dangerous. I'm going to report you to child protective services and have your son taken away for his own protection.'

"That one really shook me up. For a long time I was really scared that someone was going to show up at my doorstep and take Ben away. Most people in racing thought it was great that Ben was such a fast and safe rider; there were some people, though, who really disagreed with my letting my son race. There were a lot of mixed emotions about it back then, there's no question, but I couldn't take away something from him that he loved more than anything." Mary also lacked support from family and friends in the beginning.

As Ben was getting better at racing and studying riding technique by watching more races on TV and videotape, he came to idolize Kevin Schwantz and Colin Edwards—two Texans who were racing in World Championships. And while Schwantz and Edwards were idols he watched on TV, he had more accessible heroes as well.

"Ty Howard was really dominating the CMRA when I first came into racing," Ben says. "I really looked up to him. And the Valvoline Suzuki team would come race our local races every once in a while, and that was also a big deal. Riders like Michael Martin and Grant Lopez, wearing those Valvoline leathers; their bikes were so good. Those guys were really cool."

By the time Ben was about 12 or 13 he knew he was getting good enough to possibly make a living at racing. He also showed promise as a left-handed baseball pitcher. According to Keith, he was definitely good enough in Little League that coaches were saying he had real potential to be a high school pitcher, and probably would have had a good shot at earning a scholarship playing at a small college. By this time, however, his other sports activities like baseball and basketball had been discontinued. Racing was just about all Ben did, be it practicing on his dirt bike or at Oak Hill, or competing nearly every weekend. And it was becoming a year-round activity, with racing starting in February and going through November. During the off-season he practiced to get better for the upcoming year.

Mary said that Ben's father Henry initially had some qualms about Ben getting into racing so seriously, but that ultimately he stood back and let Ben do what he wanted to do. "Henry was very good about Ben's transformation into a racer," Mary says. "He didn't back his racing financially that much, but he didn't put up a fight about it. It had to be difficult for him, too, watching Ben do this activity with my boyfriend, so everything considered, I would say he was supportive."

"Henry is a really great guy," Keith says. "He let Ben pursue his passion even though I'm sure at times he didn't understand it. Looking back on it, Henry could have made

things difficult, but he never did, and actually, as it became obvious that Ben had potential to do this as a profession, I think he became more supportive of it."

Henry recognized that the way he'd been raised—to believe that pursuing a higher education or a trade were the only paths a young man should take—wasn't a template that would work for his son.

"Ben was a good student, but after a certain age he didn't like school," Henry says. "It was plain to see that college was probably not going to be Ben's path, and he had very few interests outside of racing. As he got better and better, I began to view his racing as an education, and, eventually, as his job; that was the life he was building for himself, and while it might have taken me a little longer to fully acknowledge that fact, he respected his craft very much. He worked at it, studied it, and continually tried to improve. Roadracing was in a sense truly a form of higher learning that he was pursuing to the best of his ability."

BELOW LEFT: Ben and Mary pose on Ben's new dirt bike. From the very beginning Mary supported Ben's racing aspirations and always had faith in his ability. (SPIES COLLECTION)
BELOW RIGHT: By the time Ben celebrated his 13th birthday he was well on his way to becoming one of the top amateur racers in the country. (SPIES COLLECTION)

LEFT: The first CMRA rider to excel outside the U.S. was Freddie Spencer, shown here with tuner Erv Kanemoto at the 1982 Austrian Grand Prix at Salzburg. Spencer won the 1983 500cc World Championship and remains the youngest-ever premier class champion, at age 22. He also achieved the unprecedented feat of winning the 250cc and 500cc crowns in 1985. (HENNY RAY ABRAMS)

BELOW LEFT: Colin Edwards won the AMA 250cc Championship and raced two years for Vance & Hines Yamaha before joining Yamaha's World Superbike team in 1996. Edwards, of Conroe, Texas, would later win two World Superbike titles and mentor Spies in 2010, his first year in MotoGP. (HENNY RAY ABRAMS)

BELOW RIGHT: Fellow Texan Doug Polen wheelies his Fast By Ferracci Ducati 888 at Mid-Ohio during his championship-winning 1993 AMA Superbike season. Polen, a former CMRA racer, also won two World Superbike Championships after leaving Denton, Texas. (HENNY RAY ABRAMS)

Keith Cherry, Mary, and Ben pose for a photo during the early days of Ben's club racing. With Cherry racing along with Ben, nearly every summer weekend was occupied by travel to races or practicing at Oak Hill Raceway, which was not far from their hometown of Longview.

CHAPTER 6 — JUST RIDE HARDER

K eith Cherry was a great sponsor of Ben's racing, and fashioned himself into an excellent riding coach, but he admits now that his brand of coaching was often simply convincing Ben to twist the throttle a little harder. This succeeded most of the time, but there were a few incidents when it didn't work out so well.

Keith looks back on it now and shakes his head at how foolish he was. There was a lot of trust between Ben and Keith that was ingrained before Ben even took up roadracing. "I had a 1992 Honda CBR900RR, and I'd take Ben on rides when he was only seven or so. I would let him ride on the tank and he would actually take the controls; I'd take my hands off, and Ben was riding the bike himself. This was a high-performance machine and looking back, it was really stupid, immature stuff, but he could do it. Even at seven he could ride these 100-horsepower street bikes and understand how to control them."

When he began racing Ben would look to Keith for advice on how to approach a certain turn, or what gear he should be in at a certain section of the track—those kinds of things. Keith, by his own admission, didn't have enough experience to give Ben the quality of answers Ben really needed, so more often than not what he provided was off-the-cuff advice that amounted to telling Ben just to buck up and go faster.

Ben was rapidly learning by listening to other racers that motorcycle suspension, tires, and so forth could be adjusted to make them work better for different tracks

ABOVE: Ben and his family were fans and spectators at AMA Superbike events as Ben was growing up. Here Mary is photographed with Kawasaki factory riders Tripp Nobles (left) and Tiger Sohwa, two of the top AMA road racers of the early 1990s. (SPIES COLLECTION)

and weather conditions. At one point he thought it would be good to try to experiment with the suspension settings on his bike, so he asked Keith a question about ride height. He was rebuffed. "I thought you got on a race bike and just rode it," Keith admits. "Who cares about setup? You're not riding hard enough if you're crying about suspension or tires. That's how naive I was."

Turn four at Oak Hill is an uphill right-hander, and Ben was having some trouble getting through there as fast as other riders. The problem was very likely the way the bike was set up or geared, but Keith gave Ben the only advice he knew how to give. "I told him to hold it wide open through there," Keith said to Ben of the turn. "Being a grown man and 170 pounds on an uphill turn, I could ride one of the YSR50s wide open through the turn."

For maybe the first time, Ben questioned Keith's judgment. He said, "I can't hold it wide open through there; it's too fast, and I won't make the turn." That was not what Keith wanted to hear. "I didn't take into account that Ben, being a little kid, 100 pounds lighter, might be going too fast to make the turn, but I told him to hold it wide open or we were going to pack up and go home."

Even though he thought he could not make the turn wide open, Ben had faith; after all, someone he trusted was telling him that he could do it. Plus, he was going to be watched now, and he had to try to make it with the throttle wide open or it would be the end of his day at the track. He didn't want that to happen. Ben dutifully got back on his bike, and after a lap or two he had worked up his nerve to try it. He approached turn four wide open. It was too fast, and he knew it, but he flicked the bike into the turn anyway, never lifting on the throttle. Both tires slid all the way to the edge of the track. Ben tried to hold on, but he ran out of racing surface. As soon has he hit the grass there was no hope of saving it. He suffered the fastest crash of his life up to that point. Fortunately, he wasn't hurt.

As Keith ran across the track to make sure Ben was okay, the first thing Ben said as he was dusting himself off was, "I told you I couldn't make that turn wide open." From that point on Ben knew that he would have to measure what Keith told him when it came to racing.

Ben was progressing rapidly. Mary had transferred him to an expensive private school when he entered eighth grade, with financial help from Henry. With these school administrators, Mary was able to establish solutions for all the school time Ben was missing because of races and the once- or twice-per-week practice sessions at Oak Hill.

Keith ordered three Honda RS 125 GP bikes and had them painted in Cherry Racing colors. Billy Wiese joined the team as tuner around the time Ben was nine. Previously they'd been using a local Longview-area tuner, and Ben's bikes were blowing up as often as they finished races. Wiese had earned a strong reputation building motors for riders like Doug Polen, Colin Edwards, Danny Walker, and other nationally known racers. Once Wiese came on board, the reliability of Ben's motorcycles was taken care of, and he began winning races at an amazing clip.

"Everybody started hating us," Wiese says, laughing. "Ben was so much lighter than the other racers that he had top speed on them, and when he started racing 125s it almost seemed unfair. He was always running up front." With Wiese's help Ben started learning more about bike setup. "He'd come in and tell me the front end was chattering, the back end was lighting up, or something like that," Wiese says. "We'd make changes to the suspension and he'd be able to tell the difference it was making."

Wiese worked with Ben until he was about 13 before taking an offer to tune for Chris Ulrich—son of *Roadracing World* owner John Ulrich—who was making the transition to the professional ranks, racing in the 250 Grand Prix class. Wiese recalled a discussion he had with Ben's father at the end of his stint as Ben's tuner.

"I was dropping off some stuff to Henry," Wiese recalls. "He sat me down and told me how much he appreciated the work I'd done for Ben. Just before I was getting ready to leave, Henry asked, 'Where do you think Ben's going with the sport?' I told him if he was my kid, I'd pour every penny I had into his racing. I told him that I thought Ben was going to be a champion. I'd worked with a lot of riders, and I'd never seen a kid with so much drive. He was there to

Ben Spies
1908 W. Hoyt
Longview, Texas 75601
(903) 758-6605

Dear Sirs:

My name is Ben Spies and I race a 125 Honda and 250 Yamaha in the expert class. As you can see from my attached resume, I have been racing motorcycles for five years now. In the upcoming race season I will participate in all of the WERA (Western Eastern Roadracing Association) and most CMRA (Central Motorcycle Roadracing Association). These races will be in 10 - 11 states and are national level. Between these scheduled races I will race locally here in my home state. My plans are ambitious but I am confident that they are achievable.

Based on my previous race record, the number of races that I will be participating in, and the amount of traveling that I will be doing, I feel that I am best suited to represent, and promote your products and services at race events. I am requesting sponsorship for the 1999 racing season. I am excited about roadracing and about the opportunity to represent your products and services in the coming year. Our goal is to acquire $50,000 in monetary support along with the motorcycle company's support and products. Keith Cherry Racing has already funded enclosed trailer, bikes, and equipment to the value of $100,000. Please feel free to call or write me at any time to further discuss the level of support you can provide so that I may meet my goals and assist you in advertising.

These are some of the things I can do for you in return for your sponsorship:

- Placement of your stickers in prominent areas of the race bike.
- Displaying of your product banners in pit area during race events.
- Periodic contact/updates with you showing race results
- Attendance of special promotions when requested in advance.
- Execution of race plan as stated

Sincerely,

Ben Spies

Ben Spies

win races—that was it. It didn't matter if he was on a 250 and was racing against 750s; he'd figure out a way to get through the corners faster and beat those guys."

When Wiese left to work in the pro series, Keith and Mary hired Johnny Hodgkiss to tune Ben's bikes. Hodgkiss was a sometimes-fiery former racer who'd become a racing director for WERA Motorcycle Roadracing. He had followed Ben's racing since his earliest days, and had once told Keith that if he could ever help Ben, he'd be there.

Hodgkiss had been working with a young racer named Ryan Smith, tuning his motorcycles. Not long after making the offer to Keith to help Ben, Keith and Mary asked him to come on board as part of the team. "We sort of joined forces, and Keith, Ben, Ryan, and myself all became a big team," Johnny recalls.

Ben and Ryan became great friends; in fact, Mary says that Ryan was like a big brother to Ben. The two hung out together, not only at the races, but off the track as well. They enjoyed hunting and dirt biking together, and they shared a budding friendship. Tragedy cut their friendship short. Shortly after becoming teammates, Ryan lost his life in a crash at Texas World Speedway in 1999.

Ben was on the track when his friend crashed. He rode by the accident site. Ryan had gone headfirst into a steel barrier fronted by a tire wall. Ben tried to calm Mary when he pulled into the pits. "I'm sure he's okay, Mom," Ben told

Ben wears No. 19 in honor of his friend, Ryan Smith, at the Miller Motorsports Park round of the 2009 World Superbike Championship. Ben won both legs at MMP, one of three doubleheader sweeps during his title-winning season. (RILES & NELSON)

her. But he wasn't. A short time later Ryan's father called Mary on her cell phone to tell her the bad news. "It's no good," was all he could muster. It took a second for it to sink in, to realize what Ryan's dad was saying.

Ryan was an organ donor so was being kept on life support at the hospital for a short period, even though he was brain-dead. Ben, Mary, and Keith were in the emergency waiting room when Ryan's family came to tell Ben that if he wanted to say his last good-byes, now would be the time to do it. It was a lot for a 14-year-old to handle.

"He was scared and didn't want to go in," Mary explains. "He didn't know what condition Ryan was in, and was so nervous, but he knew it was the right thing to do, and it was important to Ryan's family." Ben and Keith went in to say their final good-byes to Ryan.

"It was tough for everyone," Mary recalls. "We felt so bad for Ryan's family. When Ben came out of the room he was very sad, but you could tell that he had gotten some peace in seeing Ryan. He told me that Ryan looked fine, and even had an expression on his face that was calm, even happy."

Fast-forward a decade, to 2009. When Ben made his move to World Superbike, he offered Ryan a tribute of his own. "Ryan always said I would be a champion one day,"

Ben says. "So since I hit the top going to World Superbike, I decided it was time to bring him to the top, too. That's why I used the number 19. It was his number."

Facing up to the dangers of racing is something that racers of any age are often known to turn away from. Ben could have declined to go in to see his friend and no one would have blamed him, but, even at 14, he faced the reality of the situation and instinctively knew how he should handle the tragedy.

After he turned pro, behind the scenes Ben did everything in his power to make tracks like Texas World safer. He became a major supporter of a safety fund that placed soft barriers in areas of circuits that had insufficient runoff room. Those efforts paid off at race tracks across America. Three years after Ryan's crash, racer John Haner crashed in the same spot where Ryan had at Texas World, but this time soft barriers were in place, and Haner walked away from the accident. A couple of years later the steel barriers in the corner were removed altogether. Chiefly because of Ryan's tragedy, Texas World was eventually made safer for future generations of riders.

Roger Lee Hayden leads Ben in the Laguna Seca Supersport final. The race was won by Ben's good friend, Jamie Hacking. (HENNY RAY ABRAMS)

CHAPTER 7 — BOOKS OR BIKES?

By the time he was 14 Ben could clearly see the path he wanted to take in life, and it was all about racing. This narrow focus meant that other sports were falling away and, perhaps more importantly, Ben was beginning to look at school as more of a hindrance to his career goals than a help. After all, if he didn't have to go to school, he could practice at Oak Hill more, go to more races farther away from home, and not have to worry about hammering cross-country all night to make it home for school on Monday morning.

Mary was feeling the pressure from both ends. Even though he was keeping up with his schoolwork, school administrators were not taking kindly to Ben's increasing absences. Ben was complaining to Mary about school. Most parents would tell their kids to zip it and hit the books, but Mary's attitude about raising her children was unique. She wanted Ben and Lisa to be able to pursue their passions, no matter how unconventional.

In addition, Ben says that by the time he was in high school, the peer pressure to hang out, go to parties, and experiment with drugs and alcohol was weighing on him. "Nothing against Longview, but in that town, if you weren't drinking and smoking by the time you were 14, people started looking at you like you were some kind of freak or something," Ben says. "You had the extremely

ABOVE: Ben holds up his winner's check with his late grandfather, Bill Barrett. Although Mary's father owned a successful beer distributorship, he wouldn't support Ben's racing. His reason, he told Mary, was that if he contributed and Ben was injured, he wouldn't have been able to live with himself. (SPIES COLLECTION)

religious kids, who sometimes stayed away from that stuff, but not always, and then you had the partyers. There really wasn't much in between. Even the jocks in Longview were going out and partying after the games.

"People at my school knew I was a racer and they thought that was cool, but at the same time they thought I was trying to be all high and mighty because I wouldn't party with them. It wasn't the most comfortable situation.

"Plus, I have to admit that I just wasn't interested in school. There were certain subjects I enjoyed, but for the most part I was focusing so much on racing that I just looked at school as something to get through rather than something to enjoy. I know a lot of racers like me who left school early and were tutored or homeschooled now say they regret not having that high school experience, but I can truthfully say I didn't miss school at all after I left, and I never regretted the decision to leave."

One humorous story captures Ben's school experience. It happened after Ben had broken his foot during a race. Ben angered his teacher when he leaned over and described

how the accident had happened to a questioning classmate. "I got in trouble for talking, and the teacher goes, 'If you think motorcycle racing is more important than my math class, then you can get up and walk out of here,'" Ben recalls. "What makes the story good is, when I was 18 or 19 years old, I went back to the school to donate $5,000 to a cancer fund. I had signed my first big contract, so I rolled up in a BMW and handed the check to the math teacher, who was now the principal. And he said, 'I guess racing has paid off.' And I was like, 'Yup.'"

After he signed his first pro contract at 15, Ben felt there was really no point in continuing with his formal education. Ben went to tutors for a year to help him stay up with classes and his grades because he had missed so much school, but soon even that became too much of a distraction. Ben was a 17-year-old junior when he withdrew from school. He never earned a high school diploma or even a GED, and he's neither ashamed nor regretful about not finishing school. Within 10 years of leaving school Ben would earn more in the time it would have taken for him to go through college than most college graduates would earn in a lifetime. Racing was his goal, and nothing was going to stand in his way. The focus and athletic conditioning the sport required also kept him from falling into many of the pitfalls his former classmates endured in young adulthood.

A rider and friend of Ben's named Ryan Landers was a few years ahead of Ben and was also being touted as a potential future champion. Ryan eventually picked up a much-coveted ride from Team Valvoline Suzuki's support squad. Ben looked up to Ryan and was hoping to follow in his footsteps. By the time Ben was 13 he had challenged and eventually beaten Ryan on the 125s to clearly become the top gun among the young riders in CMRA.

"Ben and I had some great battles," Ryan recalls. "I remember racing at Portland one year; I was going as hard as I could, and I couldn't close the gap on him. I knew he was a pretty special racer even then."

Ryan later crashed and suffered serious head and arm injuries. It was the arm injury that would be more

Ben raced the Keith Cherry Racing Yamaha TZ250 GP bike at WERA club-racing events across the country. (SPIES COLLECTION)

grievous. The arm became weak and shrunken from a bone infection, effectively ending his racing career. "You look at Ben and the Hayden brothers and see what they've been able to accomplish," Ryan says. "I really thought I had the ability to be right there with them, racing at the highest levels, but it didn't happen for me. At least I can look at those guys now and realize I had a small part in helping them to become the racers they are today."

Another big breakthrough for Ben was when he beat one of the older local riders he admired, Ty Howard. Howard, who Ben described as the King of the CMRA, was already a veteran of AMA Pro roadracing, and when Ben beat Ty at Oak Hill it was major news, and a clear indication that Ben, even as a teen, had pro-level ability.

One early rival who was not from the Texas area was Roger Lee Hayden, youngest of the three racing Haydens that included eventual World Champion Nicky and oldest brother, Tommy. The Haydens were one of the best-known families in motorcycle racing. Roger Lee was a year older than Ben, and they had some heated races. Ben generally won most of the battles, but Roger Lee said in an interview

that when he beat Ben once in a big race, he looked back and Ben was pounding his gas tank. Roger Lee said that was one of his most memorable races.

Once Ben started traveling, his biggest rival became a diminutive and speedy racer from New York named Jason DiSalvo. Jason's mother owned a printing and advertising business, and dad Jim was a road racer. Together they ran her successful firm. The DiSalvos had one goal for their son, and that was to give him every opportunity to become a racing champion.

Cherry Racing was a strong family-type racing operation, but when they ran up against the DiSalvos, it made Keith's team appear amateurish in comparison. As Keith puts it, "They made us look like the Clampetts.

"We ran up against someone that looked to have more money than we did," Keith continues. "DiSalvo had trick bikes, a big transporter. Freddie Spencer was working with him. I mean, this was major competition. These tracks were all new to Ben, and Jason already had a year's worth of experience on most of them. But Ben was quick to learn. I became friends with Jim, and Ben and Jason got along great, but there was definitely a rivalry there."

When Ben and Jason were on the track the competition was intense, and it finally boiled over in a WERA event at a technical little track in Central Indiana called Putnam Park. Jason was lighter and faster on a 125. Ben usually won the battles on the 250s. At Putnam Ben was riding at his best and had finally passed Jason in a 125 GP race when a red flag came out. On the restart all hell broke loose.

"I don't think Jason was happy that Ben was beating him before the red flag," says Ben's mechanic, Johnny Hodgkiss. "At the drop of the green flag on the restart Jason hooked left and came all the way across the track and smashed into Ben. I started heading over to DiSalvo's pits. I was pissed, and I was going to let them know about it. Race director Jim Sublet saw what was going on and headed me off. He then went down to talk to the DiSalvos about Jason's riding. Ben was pissed, too, and he spent the race trying to ram Jason back. Jason inflamed things even more when he claimed to *Roadracing World*'s David Swarts that Ben's bikes had cheater parts. It got pretty heated."

Neither rider would give an inch on the track, and there was definitely tension between the Spies and DiSalvo camps, but Ben and Jason were still just kids looking to have fun. According to Mary, Jason's parents kept a pretty tight rein on him at the race track. One evening after the racing, Ben rode his pit bike over to Jason's pits and asked Jason if he wanted to go riding around. Ben had found a little creek that he thought the two could jump. Jason tried it and splashed straight into the mud. Ben thought it was hilarious, but Jason was mortified. His dad liked to keep all their equipment—including pit bikes—immaculate, and Jason knew he'd be in trouble when he showed up with the pit bike, both bike and rider splattered in mud.

Ben came flying back to his pits and asked his mom where Keith was. "I could tell something was up and I asked him what was wrong," Mary says. "He told me not to worry about it. This was a man's job, and he needed to find Keith." Keith was found and went up to help Ben and Jason clean up the bike before Jason's dad found out what had happened.

Mary was sitting in her pits when Jim DiSalvo, looking impatient, came by and asked if she knew where Jason was. "I told him I didn't know, and he took off with determination," Mary remembers. "There was nothing I could do. There was no cell-phone reception, so I couldn't call Keith and warn him that Jim was on the way. Someone ratted the boys out and told Jim that Jason and Ben were in the men's bathroom, trying to clean up Jason's bike. Jim walked in with a stern look and Ben ran out of there like a firefly."

Another time Ben and a couple of buddies were out blazing around the track facility at night on pit bikes. Security guards saw them and gave chase. The four of them hightailed it back to Ben's pits, ditched the pit bikes in the bushes, and ran inside the motor home to hide. They begged Mary to tell the security guards that they were asleep.

"I have to admit I fibbed a little to security when they came up and said they'd seen Ben and some other kids racing around on pit bikes," Mary says. "I told them that we had no pit bikes, and that Ben was in the Prowler [motor home] sleeping, and that I'd appreciate it if they would not be so loud because he had to race the next day and needed his rest. Of course, as soon as security left, I went into the motor home, grabbed a pillow, and started beating Ben and his buddies, telling them not to get in trouble like that again."

While things for Keith Cherry Racing were going great on the track, it was getting a little rocky personally. The relationship between Mary and Keith was falling apart. Although Keith and Mary were living together, they were not married, and Keith wasn't being faithful to Mary. Additionally, the two began disagreeing more and more about the direction for Ben's racing career. As Ben's mother, Mary felt she had the right to make decisions when it came to potential rides that might come Ben's way. Keith was Ben's primary sponsor and had become almost a surrogate father. He also felt entitled to direct Ben's career. Mary began getting her own separate hotel room when they traveled to races, and she eventually told Keith their relationship was over. The personal friction between them inevitably spilled over to the racing team.

Ben's mechanic Johnny Hodgkiss remembers being caught in the middle. "It got pretty tense under our canopy," Hodg-

kiss recalls, laughing. "I had to keep my head down and just focus on giving Ben what he needed on the track."

The conflict came to a head at a race in Savannah, Georgia. Keith stormed in while Johnny was working on the bikes and told him to load up all the equipment. Johnny recalls: "He said, 'That's it, I'm done. We're selling all the bikes and getting out.'"

This was in the middle of Ben's run at several club-racing championships. While Keith thought he had forced Mary into a position where she would do what he wanted her to do, she proved resilient. She and Johnny were able to find other bikes for Ben to race when Keith temporarily shut down Cherry Racing.

Johnny made a mad dash to Arkansas to pick up some bikes from race-team owner Alan Taylor and get them ready for the following week's event. Johnny remembers the hard work he did, preparing those machines. "One of the bikes I got hadn't been raced in years. I told Ben, 'The bikes may not be perfect at first, but they'll get better.' Sure enough, we had those things humming as good as his other bikes within a week or two."

Keith came back, and he and Mary tried to patch up the relationship, but it was too late. Soon Keith was out of the picture entirely. It was tough on everyone, but especially on Ben. Keith had been like a father to Ben, and he was the one who had gotten him into motorcycles, supporting his racing along with Mary. For nine years Keith had been there, and now that support was gone. In his last season as an amateur, Mary had to find a way to pay for Ben's racing all by herself.

"That was a tough time for everyone," Ben remembers. "Not only were we going to be racing on our own for the

first time, but seeing what my mom went through had a lasting effect on me. I think to this day I'm careful about relationships, not wanting to get too deep into something if I don't see some sort of future in it."

Mary was focused like a laser beam when she took charge of Ben's racing program. Knowing that Ben was being scouted by national-level teams, and that he was so close to finally realizing his dream of becoming a pro racer, made maintaining that focus even more important. At one point Mary was holding down three jobs in an effort to make ends meet: She worked as a real estate agent and a substitute teacher, and even took a night job as a phone operator to keep Ben's racing going.

Mary's dad certainly had the means to step in and help, but he later told Mary why he didn't. "My father had this incredible fear that if he contributed directly to Ben's racing and Ben got hurt, he would not be able to live with the guilt," Mary recalls. "And that was fine, because I understood his feelings. I had them, too, but I knew how badly Ben wanted this."

ABOVE LEFT: Roger Lee, Earl, Tommy, and Nicky Hayden (from left to right), seen here at Daytona in 2002, were instrumental early in Ben's professional career. Roger Lee remembers one occasion where he beat Ben in a big race and looked back to see Ben pounding his gas tank in frustration. (HENNY RAY ABRAMS) **ABOVE RIGHT:** Jason DiSalvo and Ben had epic battles early in their careers, but they also became good friends. Here DiSalvo wheelies on his way to winning one of two races at the 2001 WERA Grand National Finals, a race Ben didn't compete in. (HENNY RAY ABRAMS)

Ben first began to attract national attention while he was racing in the Aprilia Cup for Blackmans Cycle. Mary's involvement in Ben's racing career stood in stark contrast to other riders who were mainly backed by their fathers. (SPIES COLLECTION)

CHAPTER 8 — SHOWDOWN AT POCONO

s Ben drew closer to the age of 16, he and his family knew that a pro ride—the goal they'd been working toward his entire life—was just around the corner. Jeff Wilson, who coordinated and issued factory sponsorship for the support road-race teams for American Suzuki, was the first at Suzuki to become aware of Ben. Wilson was a former amateur motocross racer and worked in the sports-promotion department for Suzuki. Although he'd seen Ben's name in some of the roadracing publications and heard his name mentioned, Ben was still barely a blip on the radar as far as the factories were concerned.

Wilson came to Indiana and happened to be at the Putnam Park Road Course to watch one of his teams, the Suzuki-backed WERA National Endurance team, Arclight Racing. While there he walked to the scoring tower to grab some results. On the way out he ran into Mary.

"Mary stopped me and asked if I was the guy from Suzuki," Wilson recalls. "I told her I was. She told me she'd been wanting to meet me. We made our introductions and she pointed over to Ben, who was about 100 yards away on the pit road, and said, 'You see that kid over there? That is Suzuki's next superstar.'

"I said, 'Really.' I'd heard parents say things like that many times before. A guy from the 1800CrotchRocket team named Alan [Taylor] was working with Ben, and he

ABOVE: Ben races in the rain at the 1999 WERA Grand National Finals. Race reporter David Swarts could tell that on every lap, Ben was testing and learning the limits in the rain so that by the end of the race, he was the fastest rider on the track. Ben has become known as an excellent wet-track rider. (RILES & NELSON)

mentioned Ben as well, and I talked with *Roadracing World*'s David Swarts, and he told me about him, so I definitely watched his race with interest.

"I don't remember all the details, but I know I saw Ben lining up for the 600 race with a lot of the top WERA riders there, and he started near the back on a bike that frankly didn't look like it should be ridden across the paddock, much less raced. It seemed just a little rough. I remember he quickly worked his way up through the field, and within just a few laps he was up to second. I think then he had some problems—he ran off the track or something—but I remember thinking the kid was in a hurry, and on a mission."

Wilson says that while he was very impressed with the young Texan, he was a little concerned about his size. "I remember that was when the trend of downsizing of riders was really in full swing. I distinctly remember asking Mary what boot size Ben wore, and she said 11; I remember thinking that the kid was going to grow and be too big, like a football player. I was concerned about that."

Later, Wilson had a discussion with John Ulrich, the owner of Valvoline EMGO Suzuki, one of the leading race teams in AMA Pro Racing. Wilson worked with Ulrich on the Suzuki support program, and he wanted to let him know that if Ulrich was interested in signing Ben, Suzuki would be on board.

"Ben was the kind of kid you'd like to have racing your bikes," Wilson says. "He was a good-looking kid, polite, not cocky, not tattooed out. He was the all-American boy. All of that and he was very fast."

At the WERA Grand National Finals in 1998, Ben finished second in the 125 Grand Prix class to the older and more-experienced Michael Himmelsbach, beating archrival Jason DiSalvo in the process. Himmelsbach was from a racing family based in the Lehigh Valley of Pennsylvania. His father Bill was a solid professional racer/tuner who had gotten dozens of racers involved and helped keep them going in roadracing, building their motors. The Himmelsbachs would be pivotal in helping Ben turn pro.

Further, Ben took fourth in the highly competitive Formula 2 class behind veteran racers Lee Acree (first), and Brian Lantz (third), and his CMRA buddy Ryan Landers. In that race he beat several riders who were already racing in the AMA Pro ranks, including Chris Ulrich, a fast Southern California rider who had started racing pro events earlier that season and had even scored a top-10 finish in the AMA 250 Grand Prix Championship.

In his final full season before turning pro, Ben was starting to gain more attention. His local newspaper wrote an article on the promising young racer, and he was being featured in motorcycle racing publications in the U.S.

"The first time I saw an article on me it was a real rush," Ben admitted. The media attention was not going unnoticed.

Late in the 1999 season Ben was invited to race for Blackmans Cycle in the Aprilia Cup Challenge Series, a racing series featuring riders gunning it out on tightly restricted Aprilia RS250 street bikes. One of the leading riders in the series was Michael Himmelsbach. Mike was injured in the middle of the season. He and his father Bill talked it over and decided it would be a good idea to give Ben a shot on the motorcycle. They recommended to Blackmans Cycle team manager Kris Bickford that Ben be put on the bike for the final two rounds of the series. The team called Mary, and it was agreed that Ben would come to Pocono Raceway to race in the penultimate round of the series.

If there is one race that stands out as the race that announced to the racing fraternity that Ben Spies was one of the most talented young road racers in the country, the Aprilia Cup race at Pocono would be it.

"One of the reasons we wanted to put Ben on the bike was because we wanted to see if someone could beat John Hopkins," says Bill Himmelsbach. Hopkins was a Southern California racer who emerged from mini-bike racing on go-kart tracks to become the hottest young roadracing prospect.

Hopkins was 16, a year older than Ben, and was being groomed by John Ulrich for a future in grand prix racing. Over the years Ulrich's teams had given many of America's top racers their first national-level ride. In addition to running a major factory-backed roadracing team, Ulrich also edited

A growth spurt when he was 15 meant that Ben was having a very tough time fitting on the GP machines, especially the 125cc bike. In his final half-season racing the 125 he was losing massive ground on the straights to smaller riders. (SPIES COLLECTION)

As he began to grow too big for his smaller GP bikes, Ben started making the transition to the larger production bikes. This was one of his early rides on a 600 Supersport bike. (SPIES COLLECTION)

The Aprilia Cup event at Pocono was Ben's breakout race. Ben (No. 61) raced John Hopkins (No. 78) on identical machines, leading portions of the race and running wheel to wheel before Hopkins nipped Ben on the last lap. Hopkins was already racing successfully in the pro ranks, and in this race Ben demonstrated that he was ready to move to the next level. (RILES & NELSON)

and published the leading roadracing monthly in America, *Roadracing World*. He was also the person who recommended a young Kevin Schwantz to Yoshimura Suzuki, helping to put Schwantz on the path that would eventually lead to a World Championship. Ulrich looked at Hopkins as perhaps the best talent he'd ever worked with. The Pocono Aprilia race would mark the first time Hopkins and Ben would go head to head on equally prepared machinery.

Ben had never raced the street-bike-based Aprilia RS250 before, and after his first practice sessions at Pocono he wasn't all that impressed. "It was a little mean to say, but when a reporter asked me about the bike I said it felt like my [Yamaha TZ] 250 running on one cylinder," he remembers. In spite of the bike's lack of power, Ben quickly got up to speed.

Mary recalls watching the two young riders in a race-long battle at Pocono from the top of an infield building. Watch-

ing alongside Mary was Ulrich, who was grooming Hopkins for a future MotoGP career. Ulrich was amazed that Ben was able to challenge Hopkins. Ben led major portions of the race, until Hopkins dove underneath Ben on the final turn and was able to hold on for a narrow win. As the two took the checkered flag Mary recalls Ulrich looking at her and saying, "We've just watched the future of roadracing."

A reporter asked Hopkins for his impression of Ben. As racers tend to do at times, Hopkins downplayed the talent shown by a new, younger rival, simply saying of Ben, "He's a good rider. He's a clean rider."

One race remained in the Aprilia series, and it was at Texas World Speedway, one of Ben's home tracks. Hopkins, who was leading in the standings, came down, and this time it was no contest. Bill Himmelsbach had installed new pistons and rings in the RS250 that Ben rode, and he dominated qualifying and the final Aprilia race, winning from Hopkins by more than 13 seconds.

Hopkins explained the big loss by saying his bike was not running well, and that he was racing conservatively to win the championship; regardless of the circumstances, Ben had just beaten the top-ranked young racer in America by 13 seconds. Since Hopkins had raced the entire series and won the Aprilia Championship, he was given the opportunity to go to Italy to try out for the Aprilia GP team. People knew who John Hopkins was. After their pair of meetings in the Aprilia races, a lot of people were starting to recognize the name "Spies" for the first time.

As Ben continued to rack up wins, one of the issues his mechanic Johnny Hodgkiss had to deal with was the growth spurt Ben was experiencing at the time.

"We started the season with the top of Ben's head coming about to my shoulders," Hodgkiss recalls. "By the end of that season he was looking at me square in the eyes. He grew into the 250s and was doing really well on those, but he was outgrowing the 125s. He was over-riding those little bikes; he could still win races, but it was getting tougher. His size had become a disadvantage. He was growing like a weed, and it seemed like every weekend was a new ball game when it came to setup."

Mary laughs when she remembers that summer. "I was sending him off with his dad every couple of months to buy new clothes. Henry was the one who taught Ben to love shopping—and it was always at the best stores. I've never seen a kid grow so fast. It seemed like when he got up in the morning he was an inch taller than when he'd gone to bed."

As happens so often in racing, seemingly unrelated things happen that have a profound influence down the line. A tragic accident by another promising young rider late in the 1999 racing season would turn out to have an impact on Ben's future. Ironically, this accident happened in Dallas, a second home to Ben since Mary had grown up there, and Ben had spent a lot of time with his grandparents in that city.

Toby Jorgensen was a promising young flat-track racer from Stockton, California. Toby's uncle Alex had been an AMA Grand National star in the 1970s and '80s. Along with

BELOW LEFT: The Suzuki Cup is an institution in American motorcycle roadracing, so it was significant when Ben finished second to John Hopkins in his first weekend with the Valvoline EMGO Suzuki team. The 1999 season was the one where Ben broke through to national recognition. (RILES & NELSON)
BELOW RIGHT: Ben and fellow racer David Rose have a laugh after a race at Pocono Raceway. Ben was just 15 at the time, but he was already used to traveling to tracks across the country to compete in roadracing events. He raced in various series, including WERA, CCS, Formula USA, and AMA-sanctioned events as an amateur. (RILES & NELSON)

showing incredible potential in flat track, Jorgensen was also looking to follow in the tradition of an earlier generation of racers who had made a successful transition to roadracing. Toby had won 125 Grand Prix club races as a 16-year-old amateur. After turning pro he shocked the flat-track establishment by finishing second in the prestigious Peoria TT AMA Grand National to multi-time national champion Chris Carr.

A month after Peoria the AMA Grand National Championship visited the mile-long horse-racing track called Lone Star Park in the Dallas suburb of Irving, Texas. The AMA riders complained that the track was not suitable for motorcycle racing because of the thick sand base that caused deep rutting and hindered riders' visibility by covering their face shields with wet sand. Some of the top riders decided to sit out the race in protest. In spite of the objections, the National went on. Jorgensen crashed into a steel rail that bordered the perimeter of the track. The rail snapped, and Jorgensen's body hit the exposed edge, causing him to suffer terrible internal injuries. He died several weeks later in the hospital.

Jorgensen had raced with Ulrich's Valvoline EMGO Suzuki squad earlier that summer at Pocono, and did well enough for the team to prepare a bike for him for the WERA Grand National Finals.

"I had gotten a call from a tire rep in Texas [Michelin rep David Hirsch], and he told me that if I had any extra motorcycles for the GNF, that I should give Spies a ride," Ulrich remembers. "We had this bike prepared for Toby, so we got in touch with Mary to see if Ben would like to race this 600 we had at the GNF."

The fact that Ulrich was offering Ben a ride was an accomplishment in and of itself. The first contact Ben had had with Ulrich was three years earlier on the track at Road Atlanta—and it hadn't gone so well.

"I was out riding around in this practice session and I was catching this kid," Ulrich recalls. "He's going pretty decent, but I'm gaining on him. He looks back and sees me, and he keeps looking back a lot. We go down the front straightaway and we go into turn one; the kid looks over his shoulder at me, and he rides all the way up the hill looking backwards. I thought, 'This kid is going to run off the track and endo and take me with him.'

"I came into the pits and I go looking around for this kid. I see Billy Wiese working on his bike. I knew Billy, and I asked, 'Who's in charge of this kid?' Billy said, 'I guess I am.' So I said, 'Dude, he needs to not be looking back at me going up the hill. He needs to look where he's going.'

"That same weekend this kid came up to me in the pits and said, 'Hi. I'm Ben Spies, and I just turned this lap time. How fast did you go?' So the kid was lap-time obsessed."

Mary describes the first meeting with Ulrich a bit differently. "He came to our pits yelling at Ben," Mary says. "Of course I didn't like that, and I marched right over to talk with Evelyne [Clarke, president of WERA], and John followed me over there. I was quite upset, and I acted like I didn't know John was behind me. I went up to Evelyne and said, 'I don't know who he thinks he is, but this man, I think his name is John Uldick [intentionally mispronouncing Ulrich's last name as he stood right behind her], this Uldick is over here yelling at my 12-year-old son.'"

So the relationship between Mary and Ulrich got off to a rocky start. It wouldn't improve much, even after Ben began riding for Ulrich's team.

Ben rode a Valvoline EMGO Suzuki GSX-R600 at the 1999 WERA Grand National Finals. It was his first ride on a top-level professional team, and he didn't disappoint. Ben won the WERA Formula 2 class, clinching the championship in the process, having to borrow the Valvoline EMGO Suzuki to race in F2 after his Yamaha TZ250 blew up. According to Johnny Hodgkiss, at one point in that race Ben rode off into the wet grass coming onto Road Atlanta's front straight, but somehow managed not to crash.

At 15, Ben became the youngest WERA National Series Champion. He also finished second to Hopkins in the Suzuki GSX-R600 Cup event held in the rain. It was the first time Ben had raced a 600 in the rain. The successful GNF was the culmination of perhaps the most hectic racing season he would ever experience. In all, Ben raced in over 100 races on nine different motorcycles that season. Amazingly, he suffered only two crashes the entire year.

Ben celebrates his second-place finish in the 1999 Suzuki GSX-R Cup Finals riding a Valvoline EMGO Suzuki. Following Ben on the cooldown lap is Canadian Joseph Temperato. The '99 season was an outstanding year for Ben, in which he earned national recognition for his club-racing accomplishments. (RILES & NELSON)

After placing a close second to John Hopkins in the Aprilia Cup at Pocono, Ben defeated Hopkins at Texas World Speedway later that summer, to the delight of the Blackmans Racing crew. (RILES & NELSON)

Ben continued to make friends and family laugh by wearing his hair in some crazy fashion. Here, even after he became a professional racer on the Valvoline Suzuki squad, he plays around with a colorful wig in the pits. (SPIES COLLECTION)

CHAPTER 9 — A PRO AT 16

en's performance at the GNF—combined with his earlier Aprilia Cup race experience, competing with Hopkins—convinced John Ulrich to sign Ben to his Valvoline EMGO Suzuki squad. The money Ben made helped with gas and hotel expenses, AMA fees, insurance, and tutorials for school. In celebration of his first pro contract and his 16th birthday, which hadn't quite come yet, Mary and Ben's sister Lisa pooled their money and bought Ben his first car, a four-wheel-drive Jeep.

"Lisa gave up her savings to help buy her brother that car," Mary recalls with some emotion. "She was just so proud of him, and recognized the sacrifices he had made to get to that point. She was so unselfish throughout Ben's career, and always backed him in any way she could."

Lisa remembers Ben signing his first pro contract as a real turning point. "We realized that Ben's passion was leading him to a larger place," she says. "He sacrificed and didn't experience a lot of the normal things kids experience because he was so focused on racing. I did whatever I could to help Ben because he always did the same for me. That's how we are as brother and sister—complete support and faith in one another."

The plan was for Ben to make his professional debut the week he turned 16 at Mid-Ohio in July of 2000, so his racing went into a holding pattern in preparation for his pro debut. Compared to his prior season, Ben's racing schedule was pretty

ABOVE: The late Pat Murphy, PR man for the Formula USA Series interviews Ben. At 15, Ben club raced and then raced Formula USA (motorcycle racing's equivalent to Triple-A baseball) before going pro in the AMA when he turned 16. (SPIES COLLECTION)

laid-back leading up to Mid-Ohio. He primarily raced the Valvoline EMGO Suzuki GSX-R600 at local Texas races, keeping sharp by battling former AMA Superbike ace Sam McDonald much of the time. Ben also raced CMRA, Aprilia races, and WERA races.

The quiet start to 2000 was about to change. Ben was almost 16, and would race in his first AMA professional race at the well-attended Honda Super Cycle Weekend at the Mid-Ohio Sports Car Course in Lexington, Ohio. As a warm-up to his AMA pro debut, Ben raced in the AMA Road Race Grand Championships, also at Mid-Ohio. His performances in that event earned him the prestigious AMA Horizon Award, presented by the AMA to that year's amateur racer who showed the great-

est promise. Ben was presented the award by past winner Nicky Hayden. During the presentation, the AMA's Hugh Fleming called Ben Spies the perfect example of what the Horizon Award represented. "It looks like Ben could make an impact in professional racing, perhaps as soon as this week," Fleming says. "He's certainly a good representative of the Horizon Award."

"I was pretty excited about winning that award," Ben says. "Nicky had won it, and he was a factory rider already. I'd watched him coming up a couple of years in front of me and I wanted to get where he was. It also gave me a lot of confidence and some important track time at Mid-Ohio going into my first AMA weekend. I knew I was about to face the best riders in the country, but having a couple of days of solid racing there was a big help." The Horizon Award

Ben debuted with the Valvoline EMGO Suzuki team at the 1999 WERA Grand National Finals. At just 15 he became the youngest winner of a WERA National Series when he won the Formula 2 class. Here he leads Canadian Joseph Temperato in the Suzuki GSX-R600 Cup Final. It was his first time riding a 600 Superstock bike in the rain, and he finished second to John Hopkins.

(RILES & NELSON)

gave Ben the most media exposure he'd gotten up to that point in his young career.

Ben made his debut in the AMA's Lockhart-Phillips 750cc Supersport class. Working in his favor was the fact that he had had those days to learn the track during the preceding amateur races. The downside was that Ben had little experience on the 750cc bikes. Having come off a season of racing a Yamaha TZ250 and a Suzuki GSX-R600, Ben had to learn to manage the greater weight and power of the Suzuki GSX-R750 in his first pro weekend.

Ben instantly became the talk of Mid-Ohio when he qualified fourth in his very first race, sitting on the outside of the first row. Also on row one that day was teammate Hopkins, Yamaha-mounted Australian racing champion Damon Buckmaster, and Ben's other teammate, Grant Lopez. His front-row qualifying performance was better than anyone had expected, and much of the media attention during that race weekend focused on Ben.

Ben came back to earth a little bit in the final, where he finished 7th—still very respectable for a debut race. (By comparison, Nicky Hayden had finished 12th in his AMA pro debut, and Hopkins 10th.) Nonetheless, Ben says, "I expected a little more from myself after qualifying on the front row."

As the season progressed, Ben continued to finish just inside the top 10 in the 750cc Supersport races, with a best result of fifth at Pikes Peak. Racing in less than half the season, Ben finished ninth in the final AMA 750cc Supersport Championship. It was a strong start to his professional season by any standard, but especially by a just-turned-16-year-old racer with only four AMA pro races to his credit.

John Hopkins and Grant Lopez were Ben's teammates that first year with the Valvoline squad, and Ben says that of the two, he was closer to Lopez. "I was a young kid and he was this older guy with all kinds of stories," Ben says with a smile. "You just never knew what he was thinking. Sometimes he was messing with you and sometimes he

RIGHT: When he won the 1999 WERA Grand National Finals, Ben became one of the youngest WERA national champions, following in the footsteps of riders like Freddie Spencer, Kevin Schwantz, and Colin Edwards, each of whom broke through with big performances at the GNF. Here Ben is interviewed by well-known racing announcer Richard Chambers. (SPIES COLLECTION) BELOW LEFT: The Valvoline EMGO Suzuki team didn't waste any time getting Ben right to work after he was signed to the team. Here Ben is conducting a tire test at Oak Hill Raceway, the track he grew up practicing on almost weekly since his first ride on a mini-bike. (RILES & NELSON) BELOW RIGHT: Ben and Kevin Schwantz in the middle of a group of riders who were at Oak Hill Raceway to do a story on the anniversary of the Suzuki GSX-R. This was the weekend that Ben and Kevin became friends, and Kevin has been a mentor to Ben ever since. (RILES & NELSON)

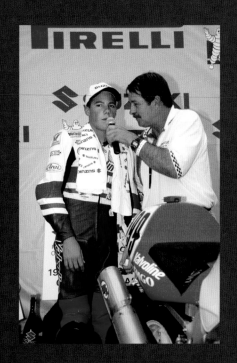

RIGHT: Ben reacts to a story Kevin Schwantz is telling him after the two rode together at Oak Hill Raceway. Kevin said he could tell Ben had tremendous potential. "I rode behind him, and within a couple of laps he was doing two-wheel drifts on this older GSX-R," Schwantz remembers. (RILES & NELSON) ABOVE: John Hopkins (left) and Ben were two of the brightest up-and-coming American road racers in the early 2000s. They were teammates for a half-season on the Valvoline Suzuki squad in 2000. Hopkins went on to race MotoGP the following year. Here the two are being interviewed by a reporter for ESPN2 after the 1999 Suzuki GSX-R Cup final. (RILES & NELSON)

was being serious, but it was hard to tell. He was a fun teammate to have."

While Hopkins was closer in age to Ben, there may have been a little more competition between the two, which kept them from becoming good friends. There were many differences between the two young riders, as well. While Hopkins was only a little more than a year older than Ben, "Hopper" (as he was nicknamed) had a girlfriend who often went to the races with him. Ben has said that he was too focused on his racing to have a serious girlfriend, especially one that would travel to the races with him.

Mary was also a constant at the race track. Ben could not drive across the country alone, so she drove with him. Many times she and Earl Hayden talked about the challenges of driving their boys all over the country to compete, and the fact that the boys had to get their homework done at the same time. Mary never wanted to miss a minute of Ben in competition, especially since she and Ben had promised Henry and Lisa that Ben would not be without family on the road. Mary also served as his manager.

Conversely, Hopkins's mother was hands-off when it came to her son's racing. Ulrich said that if they were on the West Coast, testing, John's mother would be there. "She would drop John off at the track in the morning, come back and make sure he had lunch, and then would be there to pick him up after the racing day was over. For the races she

"That first half-season in the pros was an eye-opener for me," Ben says. "The races were longer, and of course the competition was much stronger . . . it was tough to come in and no longer be the big fish in the little pond."

didn't go to, she'd meet me at the airport, drop John off, and then meet him when he got back to pick him up." John's mother gave Ulrich a notarized letter authorizing medical treatment if he needed it at a race she couldn't attend.

While Ben was enjoying racing at the pro events in front of thousands of fans, there was lingering suspicion in the Spies family camp that Ben was not getting the best equipment or the top mechanics on the Valvoline squad. Mary's impression was that Hopkins was the favored rider on the team, and that he was the one being groomed for grand prix. Mary felt that Ben was simply on the team because Suzuki management had encouraged Ulrich to hire him.

Ulrich says that he had Ben on the team because of the tremendous potential he saw in him. "I hired Ben because I saw the talent he had. We did have a plan for Hopkins, but Ben was only a year behind, and I figured we'd put him through that same program, but a year later."

The year 2000 had been a whirlwind for Ben. He'd signed his first professional contract at age 15; won America's top amateur racing award; finally reached one of his goals of joining the pro ranks; met a lot of important people; raced new tracks; and he'd gotten more media attention than he'd ever had before. He'd also beaten some of the racers that only a few years before he'd been watching through a fence, as a spectator and an aspiring racer, seeing them do what he dreamed of doing someday.

RIGHT: Ben was proud of getting his first big ride with the Valvoline EMGO Suzuki team as a 15-year-old in 2000. Here he poses for a shot with his Valvoline Suzuki bike, along with father Henry (with arm on Ben) and mechanics. (SPIES COLLECTION)

"That first half-season in the pros was an eye-opener for me," Ben says. "The races were longer, and of course the competition was much stronger. I'd been winning so consistently that it was tough to come in and no longer be the big fish in the little pond. At the same time, I knew that at my age, I had time to learn and grow as a rider. Even though I had all the confidence that comes along with being 16 and being paid to race motorcycles, I understood deep down that there was going to be a process I had to go through to start winning. I knew that a learning curve came with the territory."

One fun thing that Ben did early that summer was ride a variety of Suzuki GSX-R models with Kevin Schwantz at Oak Hill for a magazine feature on the 15th anniversary of the GSX-R's introduction to America. It was during this magazine test that Ben got to know Kevin well, and that their mentoring relationship began.

Schwantz remembers being impressed by the young rookie's patience. "A lot of people in Ben's camp were maybe a little bothered that he didn't jump into the AMA and start winning straight–away. I mean, there are a few riders in the past that have done that, and I think some people expected that to happen for Ben. At the same time you could tell that he wasn't bothered by all the chatter going on around him. Even at 16 I think he had a good handle on what it was going to take to win at the professional level, and he didn't hit the panic button just because he was finishing fifth or sixth in those races. That attitude was with him then, and you see it even today, where everything he does is methodical and at a pace he's comfortable with."

ABOVE: Ben corners aggressively in his very first AMA Pro race at Mid-Ohio in 2000. Notice that his elbows are in a normal position. His elbows-out riding style didn't start until he began racing powerful Formula Xtreme 1000cc bikes a couple of seasons later. (RILES & NELSON)

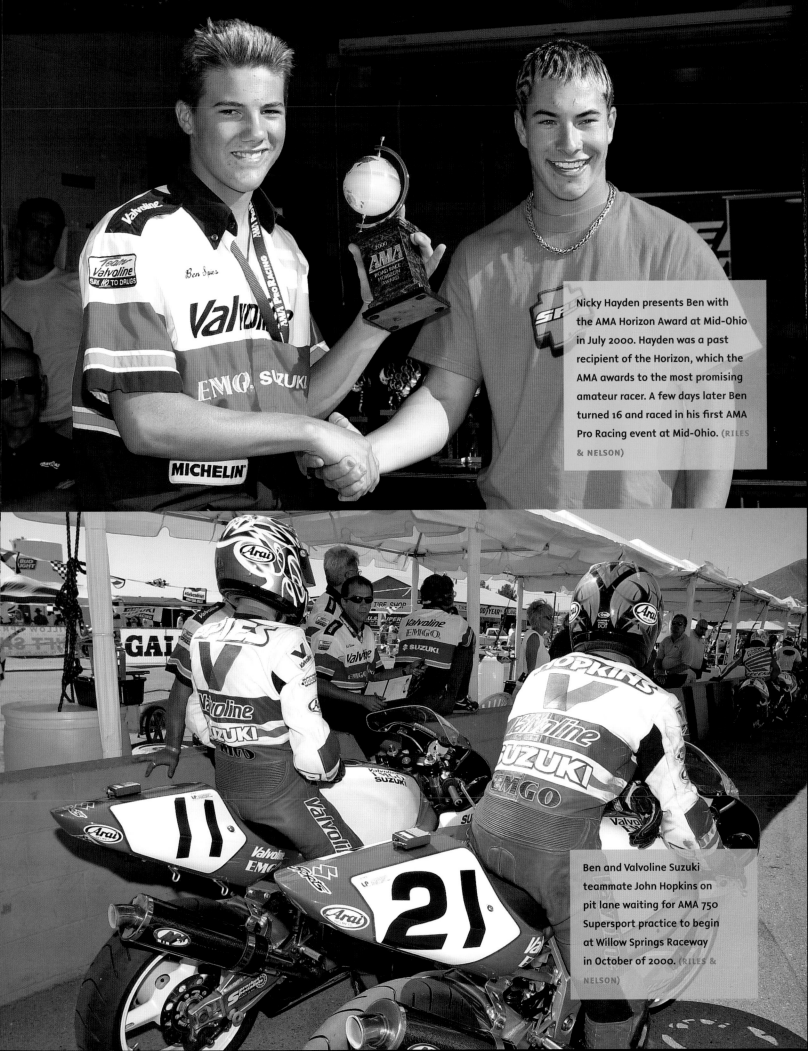

Nicky Hayden presents Ben with the AMA Horizon Award at Mid-Ohio in July 2000. Hayden was a past recipient of the Horizon, which the AMA awards to the most promising amateur racer. A few days later Ben turned 16 and raced in his first AMA Pro Racing event at Mid-Ohio. (RILES & NELSON)

Ben and Valvoline Suzuki teammate John Hopkins on pit lane waiting for AMA 750 Supersport practice to begin at Willow Springs Raceway in October of 2000. (RILES & NELSON)

Ben and Josh Hayes talk on the pit wall at Mid-Ohio in 2001. Hayes was one of the veteran racers Ben greatly respected when he was coming up through the ranks because of his methodical approach to racing. Hayes would go on to become the first AMA Superbike Champion after the Spies/Mladin era. (RILES & NELSON)

CHAPTER 10 — MOTOCRASHES

In 2001 Ben planned to contest the full AMA roadracing schedule. Now he would start to really see what competing on the entire pro circuit was like. Fortunately for him, his WERA years had prepared him well. The grueling travel and race schedule he maintained as an amateur made his professional schedule, even with testing, seem a breeze by comparison. Ben quickly proved he was one of the leading challengers for the 750 Supersport Championship, but a series of injuries in his first full pro season hampered his progress.

The year started with Ben earning his first AMA podium finish when he took second behind veteran racer and champion Jason Pridmore in the Daytona 750 Supersport race. "That was a race I felt I should have won," Ben remembers. "That week was crazy. Here I was battling for my first win, it was at Daytona, and a lot of people don't remember this, but I was riding with a broken hand. It's tough to race Daytona with a broken hand." Ben had broken his hand in a crash during the previous weekend's NASB/CCS races at Daytona.

"Jason [Pridmore] and I were racing with Richie Alexander," Ben says of the Daytona 750 Supersport final. "Something happened with Richie—he ran off the track or something, and fell off the pace. It came down to me and Jason, and he used his experience to outsmart me on the final lap and beat me by half a bike. It was good experience for me to race with someone like Jason. I'll never forget when we got on the podium after the race and he looked over at me and said, 'You're going to win a lot of races.'

ABOVE: Lisa and Ben dressed up for the AMA awards banquet. (SPIES COLLECTION)

"That meant a lot to me. I was just 16, and here was one of the best, most experienced riders in the paddock telling me he that I was going to make it in the sport."

Motocross training was a big part of Ben's routine through much of his early career. The endurance, quick reactions, and process of hitting your marks required by motocross translated well to improvements in roadracing. In the early 2000s motocross training was all the rage with road racers. In recent years that trend has cooled a bit with some high-profile injuries that have kept road racers off the motocross track. Perhaps the most famous of these was when John Hopkins fractured both ankles in a January 2004 exhibition race at the Anaheim Supercross event, which hampered his MotoGP campaign.

Ben had a similar situation happen to him. Prior to the season he had tweaked his knee while motocross training with fellow road racer, Josh Hayes. A couple of weeks after Daytona Ben joined his former mechanic, Johnny Hodgkiss, and some of his friends who routinely rode motocross at a track near Shreveport, Louisiana. "One day I was talking to Ben and telling him we were going out there to ride and he

said, 'I'm coming over,'" Hodgkiss remembers. "Here the kid was going to load up his stuff and drive all the way to Shreveport to ride motocross."

Ben quickly got into his motocross gear and anxiously sped off to the track. Hodgkiss was helping some friends get their bikes ready so he didn't get on the track until a few minutes after Ben.

"This is a long track and I was just taking a nice and easy warm-up lap," Hodgkiss said. "I came around this set of jumps in the back section and there was Ben, kneeling down and holding his [left] wrist. I came over to him and he said, 'Man, I think I really messed up.' I looked at his wrist and it was definitely broken."

Hodgkiss laughs when he remembers that his top concern after Ben's wrist injury was the reaction that Mary was going to have when she found out. "He was with me and I was going to get the blame," he says. "I was about to get the wrath of Mary."

This was just 10 days before Ben was supposed to race Sears Point for the first time. Instead of taking Ben to a Shreveport-area hospital, he elected instead to hightail it the 65 miles back to Longview as fast as he could and check him in there. He called Mary and she met them at the hospital. Surprisingly, Hodgkiss remembers, Mary was amazingly calm. Ben was obviously concerned about how this would affect his test session, so instead of scolding, Mary and Johnny sat in the room with Ben and cut up, making jokes about his predicament. "There was a cute nurse in there and we started teasing him about that," Hodgkiss remembers. "Ben turned bright red, he was so embarrassed."

When Ben got to California, the week of Sears Point, his first stop was to see Dr. Arthur Ting, an orthopedic surgeon

Ben and Mary pose for a photo in the EMGO Suzuki team pits. (RILES & NELSON)

Michelin's Walt Schaefer checks the rear tire on Ben's Suzuki during qualifying for the 2001 Daytona 750 Supersport race. (RILES & NELSON)

In 2001 Ben scored five podium finishes in AMA 750 Supersport competition during his sophomore pro season, finishing third in the final standings. (RILES & NELSON)

At the 750 Supersport race at Road America in 2001, Ben leads Jimmy Moore (No. 86) and Mark Junge (No. 571), followed by the second group of Richie Alexander (No. 25), Rich Conicelli (No. 10), and Vincent Haskovec (No. 3). Ben ultimately finished second to Moore in the race. (RILES & NELSON)

in the San Francisco Bay Area, who has long taken care of many of the top motorcycle racers.

"The motocross crash happened on a Tuesday," Ben remembers. "And it wasn't that weekend, but the following weekend that we were racing Sears." The break was not a compound fracture, but, Ben says, it was completely broken all the way through. "Broke it, casted it, drove up there, got to [Dr. Arthur] Ting's. He X-rayed it. Said, 'Impossible; you can't race—hasn't even started to heal.'" For emphasis, Ben repeats, "When I say it was broken, it was broken completely through the bone.

"Friday [in Sonoma] I opted not to ride. Saturday morning I cut the cast off and raced, because I'd just finished second to Pridmore in that race, Daytona, with the broken hand that I broke the week before on the NASB/CCS Daytona weekend.

"I had a cast on for nine days, cut it off, and that was actually one of the worst things I could've done, because now my wrist was basically screwed up until I had surgery on it."

With just a month of healing on the wrist, Ben came back strong with another podium at Road Atlanta, a track Ben knew well. Then it was to Elkhart Lake, Wisconsin, and Road America, where Ben continued to improve and was runner-up behind Jimmy Moore.

Coming into Loudon, New Hampshire, Ben was on a roll. He was second in the standings, a great position in the championship battle, with his wrist getting better every day. Then disaster struck at Loudon. A violent high-side crash in qualifying resulted in his collarbone being broken in three places. Not only did the crash cost him valuable points, but he was effectively no longer in the hunt for the title.

"This is when I was still real anti-flying," Ben says. "Mom drove us all the way from New Hampshire to Wyoming nonstop to Dr. Kieffer's, where he plated my collarbone and put in eight screws. I felt every bump in the road along the way,

RIGHT: Ben crashes his Valvoline Suzuki out of the lead of the 750 Superstock final in the final turn 11 at Laguna Seca Raceway after hitting another rider's oil with two laps to go. Ben remounted, but the win went to Chris Ulrich. (HENNY RAY ABRAMS)

and Mom was a wreck by the time we got there. Dr. Kieffer sent her off to sleep in the Prowler and I hung around the clinic. Ten days later I was racing at Laguna Seca."

In spite of coming off wrist and collarbone surgery, a beat-up Ben still had a golden opportunity to win his first pro race at Laguna Seca. He passed early leader Jimmy Moore and had a healthy lead when he crashed in turn 11 with two laps to go, handing the victory to Chris Ulrich.

"I was up by seven or eight seconds and a guy blew a motor in the last corner," Ben said. "I could see the oil trail on the ground. When I crashed I got up, and I think five or six riders crashed right behind me. I got the bike up and was still in second place. I had one lap left, but the shifter was broken and it was stuck in first gear. I had to go an entire lap in first gear and finished 16th or something like that. I had really bad luck that year."

While the action on the track was often chaotic for Ben, behind the scenes things were not calming down either. Hopkins was en route to a Formula Xtreme Championship and was racing 600 Supersport, as well. Ben was racing the lower-profile 750 Supersport series and was champing at the bit to get on a 600, a bike he had more experience on and felt he could have better results with. Ulrich told him they were going to stick with the plan of keeping him on a 750. Ben was not happy that he wasn't getting a shot on a 600. Mary and Ben also weren't happy with the bike Ben was riding.

BELOW: The AMA 750 Supersport bikes were so equally matched that the racing was nearly always the closest class during this era, which helped Ben hone his skills in heavy traffic. This is Virginia International Raceway in September of 2001. (RILES & NELSON)

What happened next depends on whom you ask. According to John Ulrich, Ben wanted to go to another team. "I told Ben he had a contract, and he was going to stick with the contract and not go to another team," is how Ulrich remembers it. "He was obviously frustrated that he wasn't winning, and [he felt] it had to be an external reason. The bikes were no good; the setup was no good; the mechanics were no good; Keith [Perry, the team's crew chief] was no good." Ben doesn't deny there were problems, but says he has nothing but respect for Keith Perry.

Ulrich noticed that Ben was slowing more than his teammates late in races and encouraged Ben to train harder and increase his physical conditioning. Ben didn't say anything to anyone at the time, but his knee was locking up in the second half of the races. It was another motocross injury coming back to haunt him. He finally found a doctor a couple of years later that diagnosed a cartilage issue with his knee. The painful knee kept him from doing much conditioning training. His doctors had said Ben could race, but running should be avoided because it could aggravate the inflammation.

In the end Ulrich felt frustrated with the time Ben was on his team. "For some reason I didn't feel like I could get the best out of the kid," he says.

After several podiums and near misses and an injury-plagued summer, Ben finally broke through to score his first AMA national victory, at the 2001 Pikes Peak 750 Supersport race in August. Pikes Peak International Raceway is a tight, twisty little 1.3-mile circuit in Fountain, Colorado, in the shadow of the Rocky Mountains. It was built in the infield of a one-mile oval and incorporated part of that oval. It was a real racers' track, and having trained for years on a tight circuit like Oak Hill gave Ben a real advantage at Pikes Peak. He took the lead on the first lap and led the entire race en route to a 2.4-second margin of victory over Jimmy Moore on the Corona EBSCO Suzuki.

"It was one of those races where everything was working good," Ben said of his first AMA victory. "I think we had a little bit of an advantage there with the Michelins. I remember before the race asking my mechanic, 'What do I do if I win the race?' One thing I'd always wanted to do was

Ben scored his breakthrough AMA victory in AMA 750 Supersport at Pikes Peak International Raceway in August of 2001. Here Ben leads the pack in that race on the twisty little 1.3-mile oval/infield road-course circuit. (RILES & NELSON)

Ben gets the champagne shower from second-place finisher Jimmy Moore (right) and Chris Ulrich, who was third, after Ben earned his first AMA victory in the 750 Supersport class at Pikes Peak International Raceway. (RILES & NELSON)

Shane Clarke (right) was a former racer and served as Ben's first mechanic when he turned pro. Clarke was not yet a seasoned mechanic when he worked with Ben, and that created some friction between the Spies camp and the Valvoline Suzuki team. Clarke went back to racing the next year after working with Ben.

(RILES & NELSON)

stand up on the pegs and wave to the fans if I ever won a race. When I won at Pikes that day I finally got the chance to do that, so I was pretty excited."

Another factor at Pikes was a new mechanic working on Ben's bike. It was the first weekend that Mike Canfield worked on Ben's bike instead of his normal mechanic, Shane Clarke. "Nothing against Shane," Ben said, "but we weren't jelling. He was a racer so he knew what was going on, but there were things I wanted on the bike that didn't get done, and the attitude was, 'This is the way the bike works best—now go ride it.' For whatever reason, when Mike came on board the atmosphere was a lot more positive and things went better, and I won my first race." Canfield prepared the bike using Hopper's settings, something Ben had not gotten all year. Ben went out and won on used tires.

The victory couldn't have come at a better time. Suzuki had told Mary earlier that this event would be the deciding race for them and their decision to move Ben to the next level. When Ben was on the last lap, about to win, both Pat Alexander (who would succeed Jeff Wilson) and Wilson were watching at the flag stand. Jeff said he wanted to stay and watch Mary enjoy the moment that Ben crossed the line

I remember before the race asking my mechanic, 'What do I do if I win the race?' One thing I'd always wanted to do was stand up on the pegs and wave to the fans if I ever won a race. When I won at Pikes that day I finally got the chance to do that, so I was pretty excited."

before he joined Alexander, who was heading to Ulrich to tell him they would be taking Ben.

"I'm not blaming anyone," Ben says. "It's just one of those things that if you don't have a great dialogue with your mechanic, or you don't feel like they're listening to the direction you want to go, it doesn't give you the kind of confidence you need. You can have the best rider in the world and, by the book, the best mechanic in the world, but if they aren't seeing eye to eye, things won't go according to plan."

One would have thought the Pikes Peak victory might have soothed some of the team tensions, but it only served to exacerbate them. Mary used the fact that once Ben had a new mechanic he won, as evidence that the bikes Ben had been using prior to that were not prepared properly.

The relationship between Mary Spies and John Ulrich, both strong-willed individuals, quickly grew contentious. Ben's future was on the line. Ulrich recognized Ben's immense talent, as did Mary, and neither was willing to budge. Later, when it came time to negotiate a contract, Ulrich said, "I would rather not race at all than to have to spend another ten minutes with Mary Spies. You want this kid? You take him, because I don't want him."

Suzuki's Pat Alexander confirmed the friction between Mary and Ulrich. "There were some pretty difficult conversations we had with both of them," Alexander says diplomatically. "I think fortunately for Ben, we tried to shield

RIGHT: Victory celebration on the cooldown lap. Ben had just turned 17 a little over a month before earning this win. (RILES & NELSON)

him from as much of this drama as we could. To his credit he never got too bogged down by that stuff. He was also just happy to be out there racing."

But while Ben appeared cool and detached outwardly, he took in everything that was going on around him. "There were some tough times, and things got pretty heated between John and my mom," Ben says. "The thing is, I think they would hate to admit it, but they're a lot alike in some ways. John knows what it's like to have a kid racing. He's dealt with all that stuff bringing up Chris. So he knew that my mom was just looking out for what she felt was best for me. She's not shy about saying how she feels and neither is John, so they were bound to butt heads."

"I once said that I was disappointed in how things turned out with Ben on my team," Ulrich recalls. "I was just as disappointed in myself for not getting the best out of him. Obviously we were right in seeing the raw talent he had. I think maybe I just started working with him when he was too young. We picked him up when he was 15. The Ben Spies we see today was in there when we got him. If we could have made that happen while he was riding for us he would have won everything. He figured out what he

needed to do, the training he needed, the toughness he gained by withstanding the psychological warfare heaped on him by [future teammate] Mat Mladin."

An incident years later would bring some closure to their fractious relationship. The 2003 AMA Pro Racing awards banquet, where Ben would be honored for winning the Formula Xtreme Championship, was held in Las Vegas on November 25, six weeks after Ben's horrific Daytona crash. Mary was still changing the bandages on Ben's skin grafts every two hours, so a driver was hired to drive their motor home to Las Vegas. As Mary tells it, as everyone was entering the banquet, Ben had Mary summon Ulrich so he could hand him an envelope. Ben asked Ulrich not to open it until he got home, but Ulrich went into the bathroom and opened it right away. According to Mary, he came out white as a sheet and glassy-eyed. Inside was a note and a check for $10,000. Ulrich thanked Mary, who made it very clear that this was Ben's decision—that she wrote the checks Ben asked her to write. Hopkins and Grant Lopez had talked long and hard about how much they reimbursed Ulrich for their crashes. Ben did not want to be treated differently, and he wanted to be straight with his debt.

"I think the note said something like, 'This is for the bikes I crashed while riding for you,'" Ulrich says. "That was the first time any rider had ever given me money like that. That was a really nice gesture. He didn't have to do that, and it reinforced the fact that he was a really nice kid.

"I don't hold any ill will against Mary. He wouldn't have gotten where he has without her doing what she did for him. When I think of Ben I don't think of the bullshit. I don't think of the times when Mary made my life miserable; I think about what Ben's done. I think about how he did it without being a dick. Mary and I didn't agree on the exact methods or tactics, but you've got to give her some credit for where he is today."

RIGHT: Mike Ciccotto (right) beat Ben at Road Atlanta in 2001 to win the first of his two career 750 Superstock races. The second came a month later at New Hampshire International Speedway. (RILES & NELSON)

Jimmy Moore leads Ben early in the 750 Superstock final at the Mid-Ohio Sports Car Course in 2001. Moore won the race, one of three in the season, en route to winning the Superstock championship. Ben was second on the day. (HENNY RAY ABRAMS)

The handling of the Attack Suzuki GSX-R1000 Formula Xtreme bike was difficult. Here Ben is nearly thrown off after he jumped some curbing.

(RILES & NELSON)

CHAPTER 11 — HIGHER GOALS

For 2002 Suzuki moved Ben to Attack Racing Suzuki, a team owned by Richard Stanboli, a former army officer and racer who started a small team in the late 1990s that rapidly became one of the leading teams in AMA roadracing. Attack Racing started its relationship with Jason Pridmore and Suzuki in 2001, and now they were adding Ben, a young up-and-comer to team with Pridmore, the veteran. Pridmore had been helping instruct motorcycle racers in riding schools since he was a teenager, along with his father, three-time AMA Superbike Champion Reg Pridmore. A two-time AMA roadracing champion, Jason would later claim an FIM World Endurance championship. Working with up-and-coming riders was Pridmore's forte, and he had helped mentor Nicky Hayden when the two raced for HyperCycle.

"We thought teaming Ben with someone like Jason would be good for him," said Suzuki's Jeff Wilson. "We thought Jason would be able to guide him and give him a new perspective on things. Jason has a way about him, and I think Ben learned a lot from him straight away. He soaked up everything like a sponge.

ABOVE: Mary and Ben in the pits during his year with Attack Suzuki. Ben says his season with Attack was a great year for him. He and teammate Jason Pridmore were friends as well as teammates and the two had a great working relationship with both helping one another on race weekends. It was Jason who gave Ben the nickname "Elbowz" after ribbing him about the way he rode the Attack Suzuki. (SPIES COLLECTION)

"I also think Mr. Itoh [who was deeply involved in directing American Suzuki's roadracing program] already had Ben on his radar, and he was waiting for some contracts to expire. The Attack arrangement was somewhat of a stopgap because the Yoshimura factory team didn't have room for him right away, and, of course, Attack was excited to have him."

In addition to being on a new team, Ben was also faced with several daunting tasks: He would be racing two classes for the first time; he was going to contest 600 Supersport, arguably the most competitive class in all of AMA roadracing, with plenty of factory and factory-supported teams and riders; and he'd be making a huge performance leap racing the Formula Xtreme class on a hugely powerful Suzuki GSX-R1000, which was as potent—and perhaps more so—than most AMA Superbike machines.

"I was 17 years old, riding a bike that had 200 horsepower," Ben says. "That was a big learning experience, and even though I didn't have any wins or podiums with the team, I was right up there, battling with the lead pack a lot of the time. Riding that Attack Suzuki Formula Xtreme bike gave me so much experience that I was able to hop on the Yosh bike the next season and win that championship.

Riding with Attack was probably the best thing that could have happened to me at that point."

Pridmore vividly remembers racing head-to-head against Ben for the first time at Daytona, the year before they became teammates. "I remember I told everyone in the press conference after the race that I thought Ben was going to win a lot of championships," Pridmore says. "I just remember thinking, 'Wow, I'm racing a 16-year-old here, and he's really showing a lot of poise.'

"He had me beat in that race," Pridmore says of the 2001 Daytona 750 Supersport race. "We came out of turn five and he rolled off the throttle. If he would have just stayed on the gas I'm not sure I could have caught him. Ben rode a mistake-free race maybe until that last lap."

There was a lot of joking going on that day at Daytona when Pridmore was told that Ben was just seven years old when Pridmore won his first AMA national. But Ben had nothing but admiration for Pridmore.

"Jason has taught me so much," Ben said of his former teammate in a 2003 interview. "Everything from body positioning on the bike, to tire wear, to setting up the bike. There are a couple of areas I still need to work on. He always complained about me sticking out my elbows when I ride [laughs]. I consider Jason to be one of my best friends. What was really cool was there would be times he'd even ask me for advice. I mean, here's this national champion coming up and asking me how I thought he could go faster through a certain section. That's the kind of stuff that really helps a young rider—to know that my veteran teammate thought enough about my riding to occasionally ask me a question or two."

Many riders who appear outwardly cocky can have deep insecurities and aren't so free when it comes to working with their teammates. In racing you hear time and again that the most important rider to beat on the track is your own teammate. But Pridmore had complete confidence in himself as a rider and had no problem sharing information with his teammates.

RIGHT: Ben riding his dirt bike during the hot and humid summer in East Texas. (SPIES COLLECTION)

Riding the Attack Suzuki GSX-R1000 Formula Xtreme motorcycle in 2002 was the first time Ben got the feel for a motorcycle with Superbike-like power. He started racing Formula Xtreme when he was 17 years old, and says the experience was a real eye-opener. (RILES & NELSON)

Ben was on a steep learning curve riding the Attack Suzuki Formula Xtreme bike. This was his first time racing a powerful 1000cc race bike, and it bit him a couple of times. This photo shows Ben and Jake Zemke after a crash at Road Atlanta in May of 2002. (RILES & NELSON)

ABOVE: This was one of the first photos that captured Ben's revised riding style, with his elbows sticking way out while cornering. Jason Pridmore gave him the nickname "Elbowz." Ben says he developed this technique because it was so hard to feel the front end of the Attack Suzuki Formula Xtreme bike. (RILES & NELSON)

RIGHT: Race organizers at the Big Kahuna Nationals at Virginia International Raceway, the final race of the 2002 season, held a party after the race that featured a charity fund-raiser. Here, Ben dances with a fan onstage. (RILES & NELSON)

"The team was a great environment for riders who wanted to learn," Pridmore says. "There weren't hostilities, and I was always willing to pass things down to people, and if they beat me, so be it. I knew Ben would be a great addition to Attack.

"The thing I remember most about that year was Ben came out to stay with me for a while. We played video games and just sort of hung out. The first time I took him training he couldn't even move for the next two days," Pridmore says with a laugh. "He was still a kid, and racing was just something that was fun. I think that opened his eyes a little bit on the intensity needed in training so you can ride at the top level." Pridmore adds, "Today, with the way Ben works on the bike, I'm pretty sure the shoe would be on the other foot."

Ben was quickly acquiring a lot of knowledge, both from Pridmore and from other riders. "I watched what everyone was doing and sort of took all that in," Ben says. "I was young and had a lot to learn. I didn't have any preconceived notions of exactly how things should be done, and I think that helped me in the long run. With Jason as a teammate it was great because we shared information. I learned a lot from him, and I think he was able to take some things from me as well."

Ben came out and rode at some of Jason's Star Motorcycle Schools; he really immersed himself in improving his racing skills and learning more about the technical side of the sport.

"Ben did one really important thing that a lot of young riders don't do," Pridmore says. "He listened. Not just to me, but to guys on the team. He was respectful of everyone, and you could just tell he wanted to grow as a rider. He was never cocky, and I really appreciated that."

Ben found out just how tough things were going to be when he stepped up to the more-competitive classes in 2002. At Daytona he finished 10th in the 600cc Supersport race. "It sounds funny now, but I wasn't upset with that finish," Ben remembers. "I mean, in 600 Supersport the field was deep. You had Jamie [Hacking], Miguel [Duhamel], [Aaron] Yates, Tommy and Roger Lee [Hayden], [Damon] Buckmaster, Jason [Pridmore], [Jake] Zemke. I was being thrown into the deep end riding against those guys."

The first Formula Xtreme race of the season was a month later at California Speedway in Fontana, California. Racing the 200-horsepower Attack Suzuki GSX-R1000 Formula Xtreme bike was an eye-opener for Ben.

"I'd never ridden a 1000 before, and the Attack Suzuki had adjustable offset triple clamps, forks, Brembo brakes, and crazy power," Ben recalls. "It was a fire-breathing bike with an insane torque curve. I mean, you look at kids coming up these days and maybe they're riding 600 production bikes. The game has changed so much from back then. The Superbikes today are tame compared to the Xtreme bikes I raced back then."

Riding the Attack beast caused Ben to improvise and work out new techniques in his approach. Among these was what has become his signature high-elbows stance. "Riding that Attack Xtreme bike was when I started riding with my elbows up for the first time. Before that I had a pretty normal riding style, but I think it was racing on a motorcycle with that much power and special Öhlins forks and more that made me change. I guess the front end had so much feel and I wasn't used to all that feeling. It felt sketchy to me, like I was always just about ready to lose the front end. I guess I started riding like that, getting in a ready position in case the front end washed."

When Pridmore saw his young teammate racing around with his elbows high, motocross style, he started teasing him, calling him "Elbows." That morphed into "Elbowz," and a nickname was born.

"I might have been giving him some grief about him holding his elbows high," Pridmore admits. "But the one thing you could tell about Ben was how relaxed he was on the bike. One of the reasons Ben is so good is that he understands the front. He rides with a lot of weight over the front of the bike and he pushes the front very hard."

In the Fontana Formula Xtreme event Ben ran a steady race to finish fifth, just behind fellow Texan and World Superbike veteran Mike Hale on the Erion Racing Honda. It was the start of a solid year on the big Xtreme bike. He scored four top-five finishes, with a season-best fourth at Road America. He finished 2002 ranked sixth in Formula Xtreme, an impressive performance for a 17-year-old kid who'd never ridden a 1000 before that year.

Things went well in 600 Supersport as well. He was in the top 10 in all but two rounds, finished inside the top five three times, and often ran up among the leaders. At the end of the year he was ranked ninth in the Supersport class, in spite of not scoring points in two rounds. In only his second full season of racing, Ben was showing significant improvement, and the Suzuki brass was taking notice.

At the Brainerd (Minnesota) race American Suzuki's Masayuki Itoh came up to talk with Ben. Itoh had been the technical department manager at American Suzuki for many years and was by then serving as an advisor. Itoh was greatly respected both within Suzuki and in the greater motorcycle roadracing community. Mr. Itoh, as everyone calls him out of respect, is a reserved man who spends a great deal of time quietly observing. As Ben tells it, to have Mr. Itoh come up and ask to talk to him was like having Los Angeles Lakers coach Phil Jackson make a call to an up-and-coming high-school basketball player.

Of his meeting with Mr. Itoh at Brainerd, Ben recalls, "I was nervous. I remember Don Sakakura [Yoshimura Suzuki's

racing boss] came up and said a few words to me. And then here comes Mr. Itoh. He was always there with his clipboard, taking times, and he has got the most stone-faced expression. When he came up to me I was scared as hell. He's so serious, and he's the main guy at Suzuki. He said, 'I'd like to have a meeting with you at Suzuki on Wednesday.' I think all I could muster was, 'All right.'

"This is back when I would not get on a plane. So on Sunday night we took off from Brainerd and started driving cross-country to American Suzuki's headquarters in Brea, California. We drove straight through and got to LA on Tuesday.

"I was nervous as hell, and Mr. Itoh, traditionally Japanese, was very formal. He basically said Suzuki was interested in me, and would like to present me with a contract. I remember he sat the contract in front of me. I opened it up to the first page, and I kind of looked at him and he was smiling. For how much they were offering me at my age, I was like, 'Where's the pen?' He could tell as soon as he saw the expression on my face that it was done. He was happy."

Not only was Mr. Itoh happy that he finally had the young rider Suzuki had been watching for so long under the factory umbrella, but Ben and his family were also thrilled. For the first time Ben was going to be making serious money. All the hard work and sacrifice the family had endured had paid off. Mary could breathe a little easier now. Although her days of working three jobs to keep Ben in the sport were a distant memory, she would discover that as the stakes grew ever higher, so did the stress of managing her son's career. The road for the Spies family was becoming smoother, but there were still many obstacles to come.

RIGHT: As an amateur, Ben had more experience on 600 Supersport bikes than any other production-based motorcycle in AMA Pro Racing, yet he didn't get to compete in the class until his third season in the series. Here he leads the pack in Pro Honda Oils 600 Supersport action on his Attack Suzuki at Mid-Ohio. (RILES & NELSON)

Ben wheelies over the crest of a hill at Infineon Raceway. "Riding with Attack was probably the best thing that could have happened to me at that point," Ben says. "It was a big learning experience, and even though I didn't have any wins or podiums with the team, I was right up there battling with the lead pack a lot of the time. Riding that Attack Suzuki Formula Xtreme bike gave me so much experience that I was able to hop on the Yosh bike the next season and win that championship."

(RILES & NELSON)

By 2003 the Suzuki GSX-R600 was outgunned by the other makers, yet Ben turned in some of his best races on the underdog machine. His victory at Road Atlanta (pictured here) remains one of his all-time favorite wins. "Racing that bike showed me that you didn't always have to have the best bike to win," Ben says. (RILES & NELSON)

CHAPTER 12 — TEAMWORK COUNTS

en had finally realized his dream of becoming a member of a factory team, but early on Ben found out that his relationship with the team's lead rider Mat Mladin wasn't going to be the friendly one he'd had with most of his other teammates in the past.

Ben would be working with Tom Houseworth as his crew chief. Their relationship would develop into one of the best pairings in motorcycle roadracing. Houseworth, affectionately called "House" by his friends—both because of his name and his physical stature—came up through the club-racing ranks, building bikes and earning next to nothing during the 1980s. He worked with Cal Rayborn III, the son of the legendary American road racer of the 1960s and early '70s, Cal Rayborn II. Houseworth then joined the powerful Vance & Hines Yamaha team in AMA Superbike. By the mid-1990s he'd worked his way up to crew chief for the Vance & Hines team.

By the time Houseworth was assigned to work with Ben he'd already worked with riders like Anthony Gobert, Tom Kipp, Jamie Hacking, Rich Oliver, and Tommy Hayden.

"It was refreshing working with a young kid just coming up," Houseworth says. "I remember Ben was shy; he seemed a little intimidated by getting his first factory ride. I remember the first test with us, and he was fast and smooth and looked really good for a first-time factory rider. After just 20 minutes of him being on the bike I remember telling Mr. Itoh, 'You'd better hold on to this kid; he's going to be pretty good.'"

ABOVE: Now with the factory-supported Yoshimura Suzuki team, Ben waits in the pits between sessions. Among Mary's many roles as Ben's manager is one that is fairly basic— making sure Ben remains well hydrated. During a race weekend things can get so hectic that riders often forget to eat or drink enough to maintain their energy levels. (SPIES COLLECTION)

In 2003, Ben was to race the same two classes he had in 2002: 600 Supersport and Formula Xtreme. His first test with Yoshimura came at Spring Mountain Motorsports Park in Pahrump, Nevada, a tight track often used by the Yoshimura team for testing.

"I was riding the 600 that Jamie [Hacking] had the season before," Ben remembers. "My times on the 600 weren't all that great. I'd just come off knee surgery so I wasn't in the greatest of shape. I jumped on the Superbike at the end of the day and did a couple of hot laps and got up to decent speed. Mladin came up to Houseworth and told him, 'This kid is going to be a rider to deal with in a couple of years.'"

While Mladin's initial impression of Ben was a positive comment made to Houseworth, it didn't take long for the Australian veteran, who by then had won three of his eventual seven AMA Superbike championships, to put the young rookie in his place.

"The first time I visited the Yoshimura race shop, Mat was there," Ben said. "I was intimidated by him because he was the dominant rider in the AMA, and really had been for

several years. I wasn't saying much as I was being shown around the shop. Mladin's new leathers were there. They had some bright orange in them. Just to make small talk I touched them and said something about how bright the colors were, and he immediately said, 'Don't touch my leathers, and don't say anything about how they look.'

"I remember as soon as he said that I thought to myself, 'This guy's an asshole. He's not a nice person.' I was just making conversation. I wasn't making a dig or anything, and he just popped off. That's how it started. Right then I knew we were never going to be friends."

Ben would have to deal with Mladin more directly in the future, but in 2003 his focus was on racing in Supersport and Formula Xtreme. There was added pressure on him now because he was on the factory machinery of one of the most successful teams in AMA racing.

Ben's entry into Formula Xtreme was not without controversy. The series had been the playground for factory-supported teams like Erion Honda, Valvoline EMGO Suzuki, and Attack Suzuki. Some felt Yoshimura Suzuki's entry as the first factory rider to contest the entire series was against the spirit of the class. On the other hand, most of the series competitors weren't too concerned. After all, Yoshimura was entering an 18-year-old rider in the class, and while he'd shown flashes of brilliance the year before on the Attack bike, not many in the AMA paddock expected Ben Spies to be the front-runner for the championship, even if he was on a factory machine.

Formula Xtreme did not run at Daytona, so Ben was given the opportunity to race in his first AMA Superbike race—the Daytona 200. In testing Ben had shown the ability to come to terms with the Yoshimura Suzuki Superbike. So positive were the results that Ben was already pitching Suzuki's race management the idea of staying in Superbike beyond Daytona.

Mary remembers a conversation Ben had with Mr. Itoh during a testing session. "Ben said to Mr. Itoh, 'I know I'm young and you want me to come up slowly through the ranks, but what if . . . what if I win the Daytona 200? Can I

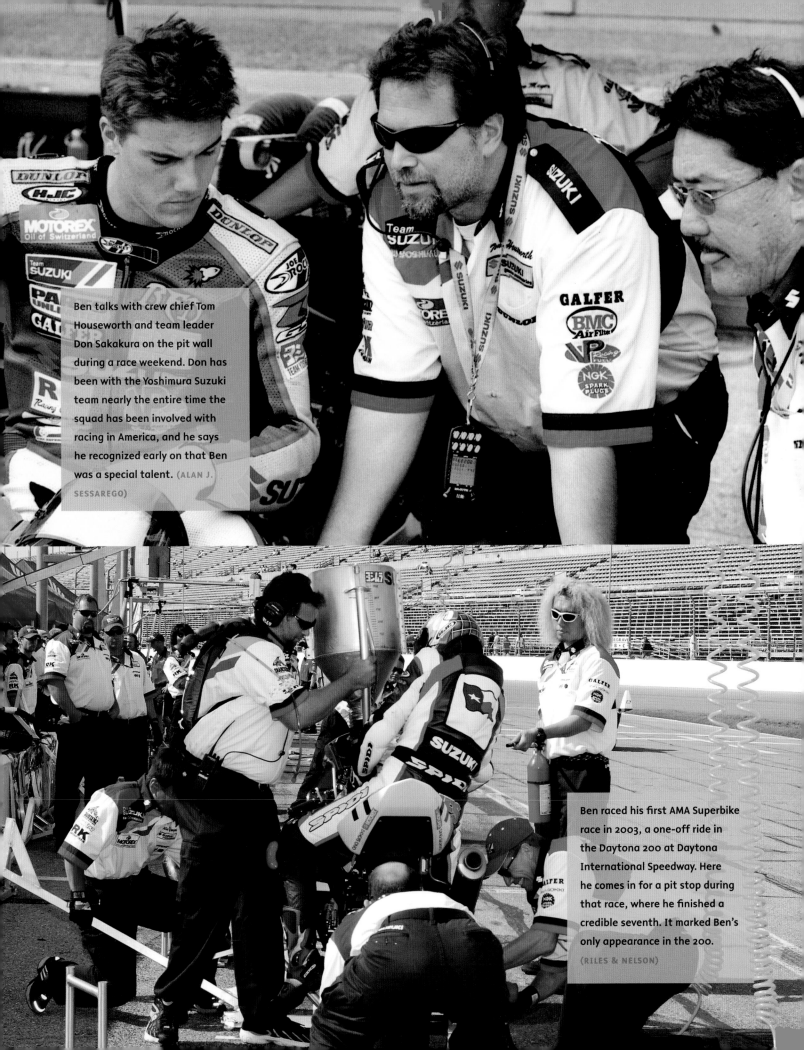

Ben talks with crew chief Tom Houseworth and team leader Don Sakakura on the pit wall during a race weekend. Don has been with the Yoshimura Suzuki team nearly the entire time the squad has been involved with racing in America, and he says he recognized early on that Ben was a special talent. (ALAN J. SESSAREGO)

Ben raced his first AMA Superbike race in 2003, a one-off ride in the Daytona 200 at Daytona International Speedway. Here he comes in for a pit stop during that race, where he finished a credible seventh. It marked Ben's only appearance in the 200. (RILES & NELSON)

The Suzuki 600 was so uncompetitive in the 2003 AMA Supersport Championship that the team pulled Aaron Yates from the class. They left Ben in the series almost as a token entry, yet he came through with some great rides on the underpowered bike, including this race at Road Atlanta where he won, giving Suzuki its only win in the series that year. Ben leads Honda riders Jake Zemke and Alex Gobert.

race Superbike the rest of the year?'" Mr. Itoh just smiled, obviously loving Ben's youthful optimism.

It would be a couple more years before Ben would get to race the full Superbike series, but he showed great promise in his debut. He rode a smart race and finished seventh in the Daytona 200, just one place behind his teammate, Mladin.

At Daytona Yoshimura team manager Don Sakakura was optimistic about the team's new hire. "Ben is a very young talent; he turned 18 this year, and it's exciting to bring a young talent to the team to hopefully train and develop his riding skills," Sakakura said at the time. "I think he's showing great ability already. We intend to build a strong, experienced team around Ben, to properly develop him, and I think his results will show in the near future. I think he's got a huge future."

Coming into the season Ben had been hopeful about the 600 Supersport class. Aaron Yates had won the championship with Yoshimura Suzuki in 2002, but things changed dramatically in 2003. Suzuki did not update its GSX-R600 for 2003, while Honda, Kawasaki, and Yamaha all moved to new designs. As is the case in the rapidly changing world of Supersport, a world-beater one year can be an also-ran the next, and unfortunately, that's what Ben would have to deal with in that class. He found out at Daytona just how difficult it was going to be, racing the comparatively slow-accelerating Suzuki. He finished 9th. And that was the good news for Suzuki. Defending champion Aaron Yates finished a miserable 14th. It was so embarrassing for both Yates and Suzuki that the team pulled him and his No. 1 plate out of the series after the Daytona debacle.

LEFT: **Ben atop the podium of the Pro Honda Oils U.S. Supersport Championship race at Road Atlanta on May 18, 2003. Ben's win on the Suzuki was one of the most remarkable of his career. Suzuki was the odd brand out in Supersport that year, but Ben earned three podium finishes on the bike, including the Road Atlanta win. No other Suzuki finished in the top 10 in any race that year.** (RILES & NELSON)

Understanding how valuable running the No. 1 plate in a series like 600 Supersport is to a manufacturer cannot be overstated. Sales of 600s were the highest-volume segment for the manufacturers, so on-track success was paramount. That Suzuki decided it was better to, in essence, vacate the title rather than have Yates race with the No. 1 plate outside of contention spoke volumes. But the rookie team member would be asked to forge on. Suzuki wanted a presence in the series no matter how bad the bike was, and Ben was assigned the unenviable task.

"That was tough, because I was really looking forward to racing a factory bike in the Supersport class, and then Suzuki didn't update the bike and it was hopeless," Ben said. "I rode the wheels off that thing and I would just get left in the dust. The bike had decent top speed, but it just wouldn't pull off the corners."

Ben didn't give up, though; instead he took on the challenge wholeheartedly and produced results better than Suzuki could have hoped. By sheer talent and herculean effort Ben overcame the lack of grunt of the GSX-R600 to score some hard-fought podium finishes at Brainerd and Laguna Seca. But by far the highlight of the 600 Supersport Championship that year came at Road Atlanta. There Ben got a perfect start, avoiding a first-turn pileup, and had a big-enough gap to hold off Australian Damon Buckmaster by 2.8 seconds to earn his first AMA 600 Supersport victory.

"I have to admit, I didn't expect to be up here this year," Ben said while being interviewed on the top step of the podium. "I'll take it any way I can get it."

Ben was just 18 and he'd won a national in the ultra-competitive 600 class in AMA roadracing—and this on a motorcycle that even Suzuki believed had no hope of winning. It would go down as one of the top victories in Ben's AMA career. He looks back on racing the GSX-R600 as a real character-builder. "I think I learned that I could still win on a motorcycle that was not the best on the grid," he says. "Winning Road Atlanta that year on the 600 gave me a big boost in confidence. If you look at the results, I finished on the podium a couple of more times that year, and that just wasn't supposed to happen."

To further illustrate Ben's accomplishments that year, no other Suzuki rider in the 2003 Pro Honda Oils Supersport Championship was able to manage even a top-10 result.

While Ben the underdog was doing wonders on an uncompetitive motorcycle in 600 Supersport, he had quickly become the key player in Formula Xtreme, starting with his win in the opening round at California Speedway. He qualified on the pole, jumped out to an early lead, and pulled away to a 5.5-second victory over Erion Honda's Jake Zemke.

Ben, Zemke, and Graves Motorsports Yamaha's Damon Buckmaster would be involved in a great three-way battle for the 2003 Lockhart-Phillips USA Formula Xtreme Series. All three would lead the point standings during the season. Ben took another flag-to-flag victory, again winning by over five seconds ahead of Zemke and Buckmaster, in round two at Infineon Raceway in Sonoma, California. But then Ben crashed out of the lead at Road Atlanta after hitting a false neutral, handing the series lead to Zemke.

Ben's Formula Xtreme dry spell lasted for four races. After the Road Atlanta crash, Ben was battling for a podium at Pikes Peak when he was run off the track on the final lap by a lapped rider. Then at Road America a glitch in the clutch kept Ben in third. The same clutch issue and more encounters with lapped riders on the final lap resulted in a fifth at Brainerd. In spite of the drought, Ben was only eight points behind Buckmaster with four rounds to go. Ben commented to *Cycle News* reporter Henny Ray Abrams at Brainerd that he felt good about his chances in the championship. "We're only eight points out of the lead, and we're going to my four favorite race tracks."

Interestingly, at Road America Ben would show the graciousness that would come to epitomize his personality. After explaining the clutch problem, Ben added that even if the bike hadn't had the issue, he wouldn't have been able to beat winner Damon Buckmaster. It was an important gesture that was quoted extensively, and showed that Ben knew how to pay respect to his fellow competitors.

In front of an international audience at the combined AMA/World Superbike weekend at Laguna Seca, Ben brought his best and motored away to dominate the Formula Xtreme by nearly nine seconds over Corona Extra Suzuki's Adam Fergusson. Ben did it after taking a chance on Dunlop's hardest compound tire, admitting after the race that it never came in and he spent the entire race sliding around. Ben also took over the championship lead for good, helped by the fact that Buckmaster had jumped the start and had to serve a stop-and-go penalty.

Ben polished off the year with dominating wins at Mid-Ohio and Virginia International Raceway. His three-race winning streak put him in a nearly unbeatable position to take his first AMA national championship in the final round at Barber Motorsports Park in Birmingham, Alabama. After his VIR victory Ben needed only to finish 23rd or better to nail down the title, leading Ben to say during the press conference, "I'll probably go to Barber with the mind-set of just chilling and gather the points I need."

Having already done the heavy lifting prior to the final round at Barber, all Ben had to do was lift the champagne and the No. 1 plate after taking a safe third in the series finale. His bike felt so good that Ben was actually thinking of going out with a win, but when the bike's front end slipped, his heart skipped a beat. "That was all it took for me to back off and just finish the race," Ben said.

Ben had just turned 19 and was now an AMA national champion, pulling away from more-veteran riders like Zemke and Buckmaster. Coming into the season he'd figured he would be competitive, but winning the title that quickly surprised him.

"It happened faster than I thought it would," he says. "Winning my first championship is something that I'll always remember. Even though I was on the factory bike, I had the least experience by far of the guys who were battling for that championship. After I won the first couple of races, people knew I had a good shot at winning, but I doubt you would have found too many people that would have predicted that before the season."

RIGHT: Ben wearing the shirt the team made for him to celebrate winning the Formula Xtreme series. It was a good thing he actually won the title. Ben was already considered one of the up-and-coming riders in America, but this championship and the way in which he won it—coming from behind against veterans like Damon Buckmaster and Jake Zemke—cemented his reputation even further. (RILES & NELSON)

BELOW: Ben gives his crew chief Tom Houseworth a victory lap at Barber Motorsports Park after clinching the Formula Xtreme Championship. It marked the first AMA national title for Ben and gave him great experience racing a Superbike-level motorcycle. Ben had to win three races in a row late in the season to get in a position to win the championship. He needed to finish just 23rd or better to take the title, so he rode conservatively and finished 3rd. (RILES & NELSON)

BELOW RIGHT: Jamie Hacking and Ben joke around while waiting to get on the podium. The two became fast friends and started caravanning together to the races and training on bicycles together in between rounds. "I was the one always pushing things and getting us into mischief," admits Hacking. "Even though Ben was younger, he was the one trying to keep me under control and out of trouble most of the time." (RILES & NELSON)

Ben hams it up with his crew chief Tom Houseworth at Daytona. Houseworth had extensive experience as a crew chief prior to working with Ben, beginning in 2003. (SPIES COLLECTION)

CHAPTER 13 — SKIN IN THE GAME

en's Superbike career was delayed by a year due to a spectacularly scary testing crash at Daytona International Speedway in October 2003. The crash was a result of a rear tire blowing out while Ben was running at over 180 miles per hour on the tri-oval section. Crashing at top speed on the banked front straight of Daytona is one of the worst things that can happen to a motorcycle racer. Fortunately, it rarely happens.

Ben's injuries, while extensive, surprisingly didn't include broken bones, despite hitting the wall. Instead it was his skin that took the worst of it. Ben says he would have traded a broken bone or two for the gruesome and painful damage the huge get-off did to the flesh of his left arm, shoulder, and buttocks. "I would have given anything just to be knocked out in that crash. Being knocked out would have been better than feeling everything that went on in that crash. I was just basically melting. I thought I was on fire." His left buttock was essentially ground off. To this day his rear profile lacks symmetry because of the crash.

The injuries and resulting skin-graft surgeries meant that while Ben would ride in 2004, Superbikes were out of the question. He rode that entire season in pain. His wounds were stiff and sensitive, and he wasn't able to move around on the bike as he was used to, yet in spite of all this Ben was able to turn in some incredible performances in 2004.

ABOVE: Ben poses with the BMW M3 he bought when he signed his first factory contract with Suzuki in 2004. Ben is fairly conservative when it comes to spending, primarily investing in land and real estate, but he has splurged a couple of times with cars. (SPIES COLLECTION)

"I couldn't believe how fast he got out of the gate," second-place Jamie Hacking says. "There was no catching him once he got the gap on us. I rode as hard as I could and just couldn't make a dent on his lead."

"I look back and I have to say, I'm proud of myself for coming back and racing like I did after the Daytona crash," Ben says. "It wasn't really the mental part of getting over that kind of crash, although that was a part of it; it was more figuring out how to ride around my injuries and still make the bike do what I wanted it to do."

When things were right with his motorcycle and tires, Ben could still win, even though he wasn't totally healthy. At California Speedway in April, Ben shocked even himself by winning the Superstock race.

"I could run with those guys, but I didn't think I could win that early in the season," Ben says. "We had a red-flag restart in that race, and we put a new front tire on and the front end was just perfect on the restart."

Ben had another great bike at Infineon Raceway a month later and accomplished a rare feat in 600 Supersport races, sprinting away for a runaway win on the strength of a blazing first lap.

"I couldn't believe how fast he got out of the gate," second-place Jamie Hacking says. "There was no catching him once he got the gap on us. I rode as hard as I could and just couldn't make a dent on his lead."

Ben capped off the surprising season with a come-from-behind win in the Superstock race in the penultimate round at Road Atlanta. Before the race one of Yamaha's mechanics told his rider that Ben could not win a race unless he got a perfect start. Ben proved him wrong by biding his time and then passing riders late in the race to take the win. Afterwards Ben heard about the statement and gave the guy a friendly jab on the podium, dedicating the win to him.

By the end of 2004 things were falling into place. Ben was finally getting over his Daytona test crash injuries and he was riding well, looking forward to launching his Superbike career in 2005. Awaiting him would be the dominant rider for nearly a decade—his own teammate Mat Mladin. It would be the start of an amazing four-year rivalry.

Ben hadn't had much interaction with Mladin since being signed to Yoshimura. The two raced different classes, and Mladin kept pretty much to himself, hanging out with his crew at the races. The intimidation Mladin doled out to his competitors was legendary. When he first came to America and battled fellow Aussie Anthony Gobert, you could feel the open tension in the air whenever the two were in the same room. Gobert, the natural talent, enjoyed partying as much as racing and didn't seem to take his racing too seriously, yet was such a genius on the bike he could get by with it. Gobert once showed up to a race so heavy that he could barely zip up his leathers. When questioned after the race about his obvious weight gain, instead of getting defensive, Gobert smiled and admitted he'd been drinking a lot of beer with his mates. "I just wanted to see how big I could get and still win one of these things," he joked.

In a post-race press conference Mladin complained of lapped traffic. When Gobert was asked about the lappers he took a sympathetic tone and said that was part of racing, and he'd once been in the shoes of the guys without much support. You could almost see the steam coming out of Mladin's ears.

Later, when Miguel Duhamel became Mladin's biggest rival, Mladin took to pronouncing Duhamel's first name as "My Gal." Another time, shortly after World Superbike ace Neil Hodgson arrived to race the AMA, Mladin walked down pit lane at Barber Motorsports Park after a qualifying session and got in Hodgson's face, yelling at him for something Hodgson had done on the track that Mladin didn't appreciate.

It seemed that Mladin's competitive fire was fueled by controversy. About the only rider Mladin couldn't get to take the bait was Nicky Hayden. Hayden was such a nice guy and never had anything bad to say about anyone. In 2002 when Hayden won the AMA Superbike title, Mladin suffered his worst season.

With Ben coming to Superbikes he admitted that he was intimidated by Mladin. "Mat had been the man on Super-

A view of Ben's ranch north of Longview, which features a small lake and wooded hills. Ben says he can envision retiring to the ranch when his racing career is done. His home there is basically a giant storage warehouse with a small living space on one side. (LARRY LAWRENCE)

Lisa and Ben with their grandfather, Bill Barrett, and father during a family gathering. (SPIES COLLECTION)

Ben doing a stand-up wheelie on his ultrapowerful 2004 Suzuki GSX-R1000 Superstock bike during a preseason test and photo shoot. (SUZUKI)

bikes before I even came around," Ben said. "He set the tone early with me, and it was clear it wasn't going to be a mentoring relationship he had with me. It wasn't so bad in '05, because even though I finished second in the series I wasn't up to his level, and he knew that."

Ben even looks back with little sense of accomplishment on his first AMA Superbike victory that came at California Speedway in April of 2005. "That's one where Mat had problems," Ben is quick to point out. In that race Mladin had a seven-second lead late in the race when his bike experienced clutch problems and forced him out. Still, Ben had to overcome a great three-way battle with teammate Aaron Yates and Ducati's Neil Hodgson to win the race.

Early in 2005 Ben was generally finishing third or fourth behind teammates Mladin and Aaron Yates, but as the season progressed he got more and more comfortable on the Superbike, and finished as runner-up five out of the final eight races. Ben remembers some of the most memorable moments for him that year involved watching Yates regularly pull off the impossible.

"Aaron's a good guy, and we spent a lot of time together as teammates working out of the same 18-wheeler," Ben recalls. "I've seen that guy do some stuff on a motorcycle that just blew my mind. Everybody who races has seen a lot of cool and crazy stuff happen on the track, but the number of crazy things Aaron's done and gotten away with . . . he hasn't always gotten away with it, but I'm amazed at how often he did.

"We were at Brainerd and we came out of turn three, a right-hander, and he just kind of snuck off the outside of the track on the exit. His rear tire was out in the dirt, and there was a little bit of a lip and his front tire was still on the track. That lip wouldn't let his rear tire back on the track, but he never even breathed it. He carried it an easy 50 yards, two full seconds like that. I couldn't believe it. Then there have been times I've seen him come into corners full-lock

sideways, smoking the tire, and then it hooks and he's got the front wheel in the air with his leg dangling off to the side. He's done some pretty amazing, acrobatic-type stuff."

Ben also learned by watching Mladin when he could in '05. "Unlike Aaron, Mat was always a more precise rider," Ben says. "He's precise, but at the same time very aggressive on the bike. There were times when I'd follow him through a section and he'd do something and it didn't look spectacular, but he'd put some distance between us. I was like, 'I've got to figure out how he did that.' He never blew my mind with some crazy slide or something. He was just fast, never out of shape, just fast."

One teammate who Ben felt was underappreciated was Tommy Hayden. "Tommy's quiet and really laid-back. He's a perfectionist, and he's always fiddling with his equipment or his helmet because it has to be just right. A lot of people have the wrong impression of him. Sometimes he'll sit there and come out with these one-liners and it's so funny, one, because it's Tommy, and two, you don't expect it.

"When it comes to talent, Tommy is very talented. I saw him do things on a bike I couldn't believe, but he's just more conservative. He won't push past the limits, and I like that

RIGHT: Ben in a preseason PR photo showing him with his 2004 livery—a GSX-R1000 Superstock (white and blue) machine and the GSX-R600 Supersport bike in yellow. This photo was taken on pit lane of California Speedway. (SUZUKI)

about him. I try to be like that too most of the time. He's won titles, even though he's never won a Superbike title. He's a lot more talented than the results sheet shows."

Ben finished 2005 as the second-ranked rider in AMA Superbike, behind Mladin, but he says at that point there was a major gulf between the two. "He was just better than me at that point," Ben admits. "That was my first year on a Superbike and things got better and better as the season went on, but Mat was at the top of his game, and I was just getting started." The turning point for Ben came during the off-season.

"I was thinking about it a lot," Ben remembers. "And I thought, 'Who is Mat Mladin?' Yeah, he was a great motorcycle racer and a rider who used his mouth a lot. I'm not saying that he couldn't back it up, but talk is talk, and that's all it is. It's not like we were going to get in a boxing ring and go 12 rounds. The talk only matters if you let it bother you. He can say something, or I can say something, and that

ABOVE: Ben answers questions during a press conference at Barber Motorsports Park in 2005, with his Yoshimura Suzuki teammates Mat Mladin and Aaron Yates in the background. Until this new Suzuki era, when the team possessed so much talent, it was a rarity for any one manufacturer to sweep an AMA Superbike podium. (LARRY LAWRENCE)

doesn't make it true. Even if it is true, the only way it can bother you is if you let it.

"I decided right there that no matter what he did or said that I was just going to let it roll off. I was going to concentrate on being the best rider in the best shape and focus on myself, not someone else.

"The off-season between 2005 and '06, I trained like I never had before, focused on being as strong and fit as I could be. I was ready to go when 2006 came around. I came out swinging."

Ben is sandwiched between Mat Mladin (No. 1) and Neil Hodgson (No. 100) at the start of a Superbike race at Barber Motorsports Park in 2005. The addition of Hodgson, a former World Superbike Champion, to the AMA series spoke to the depth of talent found in American Superbike racing in the early to mid-2000s. (LARRY LAWRENCE)

Ben dives into a turn at Barber Motorsports Park under heavy braking despite a steep lean angle, which is normally a recipe for losing the front end. But, as Ben recalls, "I had so much confidence with those Suzuki Superbikes that I did things on them that weren't exactly by the book." (LARRY LAWRENCE)

Ben (left) and Mladin fought this closely for the entire season-opening Daytona Superbike race in 2006. Mladin used his experience to take a narrow victory, but Ben realized during this race that he could run with Mladin. "For the first time I had the speed to run with Mat, and that felt great," he recalls. (HENNY RAY ABRAMS)

CHAPTER 14 — PREPARATION = RESULTS

he first Superbike race of 2006 was at the famous Daytona International Speedway. In an effort to keep the tire-shredding Superbikes from doing just that, the Superbike race had been demoted from the featured Daytona 200 to a support race a year earlier. Rather than a 68-lap, two-hour race, it was a 15-lap sprint.

No matter how hard Daytona tried to pump up the grand old 200-mile race, the fans were still primarily interested in the Daytona Superbike race. However, based on his 2005 performance, no one really expected Mat Mladin's dominance to be challenged. Mladin's total control had almost thrown the series into a lull. That all changed in the Daytona Superbike race. It was obvious that Ben's off-season training and learning from the previous season had paid off.

Daytona proved to be epic. Mladin and Ben battled the entire way. Mladin led most of the laps, but Ben led across the line a couple of laps in the middle of the race. Regardless of who was leading, it was obvious that no one was going to get away, and typical of Daytona, the race would come down to the last lap. On the final lap Mladin led, and it appeared that Ben would be in the perfect position to make the classic Daytona slingshot draft to win. But the veteran Mladin had a trick up his sleeve: As the two exited the chicane for the final time, Mladin suddenly chopped the throttle on his Suzuki Superbike. Ben saw what was happening, but decided to try to simply outrun his teammate around the banking to the line. It wasn't going to happen. Mladin played a perfect hand and was able to set in behind Ben's bike and take advantage of the slipstream created by Ben's bike, build up rpms, and make the draft pass just before the finish line to win by 0.032 seconds.

Ben shook his head, realizing he'd been snookered. Even though he wasn't happy he'd lost the race, there was something else on his mind during the cooldown lap.

- -

ABOVE: **Ben and Lisa share a moment on the pit wall.** (SPIES COLLECTION)

BELOW: At the California Speedway Ben was joined by his father Henry and sister Lisa. Henry often worked behind the scenes as a trusted advisor to Ben and Mary. (SPIES COLLECTION)

"I realized I could run with him," Ben said. "For the first time I had the speed to run with Mat, and that felt great. All the work I'd done in the off-season had paid off. I was really excited even though I finished second. I couldn't wait to get to the next race."

A funny thing happened in Daytona's media center after the race. As all the writers and photographers gathered to file their stories and photos, Tom Riles, the dean of American roadracing photographers, told anyone who would listen that the Mladin era was over. It didn't make sense. Mladin had just won the race, a few of his fellow journalists replied, but Riles, who had photographed all the American road-racing greats—from Kenny Roberts, Freddie Spencer, and Eddie Lawson to Wayne Rainey and Kevin Schwantz—saw something through his lens that the others hadn't: Ben had the measure of Mladin. He was riding comfortably at the pace they were going, and Mladin was racing on the edge. Riles's observation proved prophetic.

Starting at Barber Motorsports Park a little over a month later, Ben went on one of the most amazing runs in the history of AMA Superbike. He won six races in a row and built a lead in the championship that would prove insurmountable. It all started with Ben's first Superbike pole at Barber.

"I'd caught Mat off guard," Ben says with pride. "Even from Daytona I knew I had the chance to win the championship. Then when I won the pole at Barber, stopping a streak of something like 10 or 11 straight poles, that confirmed it."

Ben's remarkable pole streak was in fact 11—all 10 races in 2005, and the first race of 2006.

Indeed, Ben not only put an end to Mladin's record pole-win streak, but he also set a new track record in the process. In the first race of the doubleheader weekend at Barber, Ben was thrilled to beat Mladin head-to-head for the first time. "That was the breakthrough," he said later. Then Ben swept the doubleheader and Mladin crashed. A red flag saved the day for Mladin, and he was able to salvage third, but for the first time fans and racing pundits were beginning to see what photographer Riles had witnessed through the barrel of a telephoto lens at Daytona. Perhaps the Mladin era *was* over, and the young 21-year-old Texan was the next generation stepping up to begin his own legacy.

It was interesting to watch Mladin's reaction to getting beaten by his teammate. The oft-cantankerous Aussie does not take losing well; it's one of the reasons he was such a great champion. The post-race statements evolved. At first Mladin often cited a wrong tire choice or other issues with his motorcycle. He was gracious in saying that Ben was riding great after Ben pulled away from him at California Speedway; but cracks were developing, and Mladin's frustrations sometimes boiled over. In addition to the verbal confrontation with Neil Hodgson at Barber, he reacted angrily to a question during a press conference at California Speedway. When asked about losing for the third straight time he shot back, sarcastically, "Well, it's over, isn't it? I guess I should shoot myself."

While the action on the track was blazing hot, the off-track drama was getting even more heated. Mladin was pulling out all the stops in trying to get a psychological advantage on Ben.

"It wasn't just with me," Ben said of Mladin's psych job. "He would make little snide remarks to my buddies, crew members, girlfriends—anyone who was around me. He was constantly trying to create drama." One example was the kind of quotes Mladin gave to the press. To a reporter from the *Columbus Dispatch,* Mladin contrasted himself with Ben, saying: "He's 22 years old, I'm 34; he still has his mom hanging around wiping his bum, and I haven't had that luxury since I've been a professional racer."

A detailed look at Ben's 2006 Yoshimura Suzuki GSX-R600 Supersport machine. (SUZUKI)

The classic "Elbowz" style on one of the many elevation changes at the Mid-Ohio Sports Car Course. Ben beat Mladin in the first race by 5.7 seconds, and by 4.256 seconds in the second race, to move closer to his first AMA Superbike Championship. (HENNY RAY ABRAMS)

The start of Saturday's Superbike race at Mid-Ohio in 2006, and Ben's already in the lead. He would dominate both races that weekend and leave Ohio with a 45-point lead, with only three race meetings remaining in the season. (HENNY RAY ABRAMS)

Kevin Schwantz conveys something to do with cornering on the pit wall at Fontana. (HENNY RAY ABRAMS)

The dirty tricks continued. Ben's girlfriend at the time had done a lot of modeling. Someone came across some nude photos of her, and Mladin and his crew used one of the photos as a screensaver on their laptops at the track. At Road Atlanta Mladin's crew put grease on the steering wheel of Mary's golf cart, so when Ben's chiropractor went to drive it, he got dirty grease all over his hands. Even worse, he slipped and hurt his wrists. Mary saw no humor in this as she took over the wheel and was herself covered with grease. "I called [American Suzuki vice president] Mel Harris and said he could pay for damages forthcoming with his drama queen from Australia," Mary says.

Some of these tricks could be considered pranks, but it was this type of behavior that Mladin and his crew were famous for—getting into the heads of Mat's competitors.

It all came to a head at Barber Motorsports Park. According to Mary, Mladin told a friend of Mary's that she needed to move away from where she was standing at the team's transporter. It was just another of Mat's intimidation attempts, but Mary went ballistic. She and Mat got into an open confrontation, and Mary threatened to call the police and slap a restraining order on Mladin, meaning he would not be able to compete in any race.

The next altercation was at Infineon Raceway. When Ben showed up to the team's pit area, Mladin yelled over to Ben: "If you don't shut your mother up, then I will." Ben asked him what his problem was, and Mladin responded, "She is telling everyone I have special parts."

"At that point I lost it," Ben recalls, adding that he pushed a picnic table toward Mat. "I didn't care if I got DQ'd or got my ass whipped—I was going to put one shot in. Mat's good at spinning up riders and letting their emotions get to them. He did that with Ben Bostrom when Ben was dating [model] Leeann [Tweeden]. They were battling and Mat brought her into the conversation. He's good at playing head games, and that day I let my emotions get to me, and I wanted to take his head off."

Mat tried to soothe Ben with a "Hey, wait—settle down," but Ben kept coming and thumping the picnic table into Mat's pit area. Ben said he realized he had to stop or the crews would take it to the ground. It was a miserable feeling, and the hardest thing for Ben to do was to stop the anger.

When Mary returned, Ben told House not to say anything. "I slammed my visor down and took off," he says. "Mom asked House what had happened, because Don Sakakura came up to her and shook her hand and said, 'It's about time.' House said, 'Well, I can't say anything.' Mom started cracking from no sleep, race weekend, stress because her dad was dying—and House assured her it was nothing about the bike." He added, "She has nothing for Mladin, nothing at all." But on that weekend, Ben had something for Mladin; he got his revenge by winning both races of the doubleheader weekend.

It was obvious to anyone around that the tension between the teammates was growing. Some feared that it might spill over onto the race track. John Ulrich saw what was going on and questioned American Suzuki bosses.

Ulrich recalls: "I said to Suzuki's Pat Alexander one time, 'Why don't you guys make Mladin back off, man? This is bullshit.' And they said 'Why? It just fires Ben up, and he'll go faster. It's great.' I said, 'What are you talking about? It's not great. If this were an office or something, they'd all be fired.' They would never address it, which is something I never understood."

Regardless of the continual psychological warfare that Mladin and his crew used to get at Ben, it wasn't succeeding. Ben says his sweep at Infineon in May of that year was significant because it was the first time he'd led Mladin flag to flag.

"In the other races I followed him for a while and then made my move," Ben explains. "At Infineon I controlled the race from the front, and that was a big step for me. I monitored my pit board and when the gap closed a little, I just stepped it up."

At Infineon Ben tied the AMA Superbike record of six consecutive wins set by Miguel Duhamel 11 years earlier. "Ben's riding terrific, and he's a great guy," Duhamel said at Infineon. "If he goes on to beat my record, then that's great, because I think he's good for the sport." Then Miguel paused and deadpanned, "But I don't want him to do it."

Mladin came back with a sweep at Road America, but Ben minimized the damage to his points lead by finishing second in both races. Then the series went to Miller Motorsports Park, a new state-of-the-art track in Utah. There Ben demonstrated a skill that would characterize his Superbike racing career: learning tracks quickly. Ben figured the way around the new track better than anyone else, scored the pole, and went on to win one of the pair of races, while Honda's Jake Zemke won the other. The Spies/Mladin battle would rise to such levels that Zemke's victory would prove to be the last time someone other than Ben or Mladin would win an AMA Superbike race for almost three years.

Ben's international exposure got a major boost when he ran away with the Superbike win at the Laguna MotoGP weekend. It was only his second year on a Superbike, and the GP crowd probably took notice of the young American for the first time. Ben also got a major boost in the championship chase because Mladin was dealing with an illness and could only manage a sixth-place result.

Mid-Ohio really broke the championship wide open. There Ben dominated both races and stretched his series lead to 45 points. Even though there were five races to go, Ben had a big-enough lead that the championship was effectively his to lose. It was at Mid-Ohio that Mladin, for the first time, began talking more about the following year than the current championship.

Being a realist, Mladin said after Mid-Ohio, "The championship is essentially almost out of reach. We need to start thinking about how we're going to bridge the gap for next year, and that's what we're doing in these races, trying a few different things."

Mladin even joked about the situation, telling Ben's crew chief Tom Houseworth that he had a lot more money than Ben and he'd bribe Ben to stop winning. The money thing wouldn't be a problem for Ben, though. A week after Mid-Ohio he re-signed with Suzuki for two more seasons. To Mr. Itoh, Ben Spies was the future. However, according to Mary, Mel Harris admitted that he thought Ben's winning was a fluke the first time, and that he regretted the contract he'd agreed to with her, putting him at odds with Mr. Itoh.

That contract made Ben a wealthy man. Some pundits were surprised Honda hadn't pursued Ben harder. Honda was used to winning, it obviously had a competitive motorcycle, and one of its main riders, Duhamel, was quickly approaching 40.

"I talked to other teams, but I was happy with Suzuki," Ben explained. "I knew they had a great motorcycle, and I was on a big winning streak. I didn't want to jeopardize that. Plus, they were already talking to me about the possibility of MotoGP, so that was a big factor too."

Ben also reached 10 wins in 2006. It was just one win away from tying the all-time single-season AMA Superbike win record held by Mladin, but he wouldn't quite get there. A violent high-side crash in qualifying at Virginia International Raceway in August broke his hand. He wouldn't win another race that year, but even with the injured hand he was able to finish out the season with three runner-up finishes in the final five rounds, to clinch his first AMA Superbike Championship.

"That was an amazing feeling," Ben remembers of winning the title. "I screwed up there a little at the end, breaking my hand and sort of limping home to the title, but it was still hard to believe what I'd accomplished. That year began with no one expecting Mat to be challenged, and we came out and just got on a roll.

"It was funny, because I knew that we'd sort of caught Mat by surprise. He may have gotten a little complacent after winning his championships the way he did. I knew at the end of 2006 that I would have my work cut out for me. The 2007 season was going to be even tougher, and I went to work right away, preparing for the upcoming season."

The torch had seemingly been passed from Mladin to Ben in terms of being the best rider in the American championship. But his defeat at Ben's hands only hardened Mladin's already-steely resolve. He would go back to Australia and prepare like never before, setting up an epic battle in 2007 that would ultimately be considered one of the best in AMA Superbike history.

Mladin (left) won the season finale at Mid-Ohio, but with a measured ride to seventh place—his worst finish of the year, and only his second non-podium—Ben clinched the number-one plate. The title would go back to Texas by 8 points, 649 to 641. (RILES & NELSON)

The team that would win three AMA Superbike Championships celebrates after the Mid-Ohio double. Tom Houseworth (third from left) continues to be Ben's crew chief in his MotoGP career, while Greg "Woody" Wood (left) joined Ben and House during his World Superbike season, and has stayed on ever since. (RILES & NELSON)

The joy can be seen in Ben's face after he beat Honda's Miguel Duhamel to win his first Daytona Superbike race starting off the 2007 season. Mladin crashed, remounting to finish 10th, and certain to strike back at the next opportunity. (HENNY RAY ABRAMS)

CHAPTER 15 — THE CLOSEST SUPERBIKE BATTLE

The 2007 season couldn't have started off any better for Ben. He won the Daytona Superbike opener, watching Mladin crash and eventually finish 10th. Winning the Daytona race was prestigious, but all Ben could think about was the points he'd gained for the win. Prestige and history could be enjoyed later, Ben told the press. For now he was focused on defending the No. 1 plate on his motorcycle.

As part of the publicity leading up to Daytona, Ben was featured in *USA Today*. Articles in mainstream publications were proving that Ben's popularity was beginning to reach beyond motorcycle roadracing devotees. Being the American racing champion at just 22 was a major accomplishment, and the national press was starting to pay attention.

Across the country in Los Angeles, Lisa learned of her brother's Daytona victory. She went down to a shop that Ben liked to visit when he was in LA and she bought a pair of cufflinks with Ben's name on them.

"I talked to him after he won Daytona, and I told him I just knew he was going to win the championship that year," Lisa recalls. "He said, 'How do you know I'm going to win?' And I told him, 'Because you just won Daytona, and I know you; you've never lost. I've got something for you, and I'm going to send it to Mom, and when you win the championship and she hands you that box, I just want you to know I bought it today.'"

After his Daytona crash Mladin came back with a vengeance, scoring a sweep at the next race meeting at Barber Motorsports Park, including the Saturday race that

ABOVE: **Ben and a friend play-riding on mini-bikes at Ben's ranch north of Longview. The expansive ranch is a place where Ben likes to go with friends to relax and blow off steam.**
(DAVID SWARTS)

saw Ben and Mladin duel wheel-to-wheel the entire race. After the Alabama weekend Mladin had pulled to within eight points of Ben, and you could tell Mat had a gleam in his eye. It was obvious he'd worked hard to become fitter and leaner, and his team had made their bike a better machine. He also downplayed his 2006 loss to Ben.

"I don't think I deserved to win the championship," he said. "My head and heart weren't in it. The best rider is going to win this year, and we'll see who that ends up being, because I'm not going to leave anything out there. I'll give everything I've got. If I come out on top, good; if Ben does, he deserves it fully."

"I knew I was going to have to step up my game," Ben says.

An interesting thing happened at Barber that not many people noticed. On the cooldown lap Ben pulled up to Mladin and gave him a congratulatory pat on the back. Mladin's response was totally unexpected. "I don't know if he was having a raging moment or what," Ben said later. "I was trying to congratulate him, and he sort of punched me in the shoulder. I was like, 'You know what? That was a dick move, but everybody saw it.' I came over to shake his hand and he's going to act like that. I was thinking, 'What does that even mean?' Something was not right with the guy."

That small, largely unnoticed gesture set the tone for what would become another very adversarial season between the two rivals.

A week later at California Speedway the battle between the two escalated. A dynamic race on Saturday saw Ben and Mladin bang into one another repeatedly with reckless abandon for the first 10 laps, before Ben moved around Mladin and simply checked out. He put a one-second gap on his teammate in a single lap. From there Ben pulled away to win by nearly seven seconds. The next day Mladin pulled out to a three-second lead before Ben gritted his teeth and chased down his rival. On the last lap Ben was tucked right behind Mladin, hoping for a draft move before the finish line, but Mladin was able to get just a little better drive coming onto the front straightaway and held Ben off by a few inches.

As intense as their rivalry was, the Fontana races were one of the few times that the two really raced wheel-to-wheel for any length of time. Often one had a better setup than the other, and tight battles were the exception rather than the rule.

At Infineon Raceway the momentum clearly went to Mladin. He won both races to tie Ben in the standings. Ben also crashed at Infineon and destroyed his bike. The bad luck seemed to carry over to the next race at Road America, where Ben crashed again and injured his leg, got a concussion, and lost to Mladin for the fourth straight time, to lose the series lead. But Ben rallied in Sunday's race in the rain, running up to a 16-second lead before slowing late in the race. Jamie Hacking found a way to help his buddy by beating Mladin for second, giving Ben a precious cushion of a few more points in his lead leaving Road America.

During the press conference after the race, Mladin even found a way to take a dig at Ben and Jamie, even though they'd both just beat him. "The unfortunate thing for people that are good in the rain is that most days are sunny," he said.

A few weeks later in the Utah desert, Ben scored a sweep at Miller Motorsports Park. The championship might have been blown wide open that weekend. On Sunday's race Mladin crashed while being chased by Ben. The red flag came out when it appeared that Mladin was badly hurt, but after being driven back to the paddock by an ambulance, Mladin emerged and jogged to his pit, where his crew miraculously got the bike repaired in time for the restart. Instead of finishing with no points, Mladin was able to bravely ride to a gritty fourth-place finish. Being able to restart and finish the race meant that instead of being 45 points ahead, Ben left Utah with just an 18-point lead in the standings.

The big Laguna Seca MotoGP weekend was next up. Ben made it clear in a press conference leading up to the race that MotoGP was where he wanted to be, and with the most influential people in international roadracing watching, he proceeded to go out and turn in a winning audition. Ben pulled out all the stops and motored away to a convincing five-second victory over Mladin. The managers of the GP paddock were becoming more convinced that

Ben wheelies the Yoshimura Suzuki out of a corner at Road Atlanta in September of 2007. Ben says his 2007 AMA Superbike Championship was his favorite in America; that was the year he beat teammate Mat Mladin by a single point. (LARRY LAWRENCE)

The 2007 season couldn't have started any better, with Ben beginning the defense of his title with a win, while Mladin crashed, finishing 10th. It was Ben's first Superbike win at Daytona, but the points were what mattered most.

(HENNY RAY ABRAMS)

With Mary and mentor Kevin Schwantz looking on, Ben makes it clear who's number one after winning the 2007 AMA Superbike Championship in the finale at Mazda Raceway Laguna Seca.

(RILES & NELSON)

Ben had potential on the world stage, and Ben's name was frequently being mentioned as a future MotoGP rider.

"I'm trying 100 percent at every race, but at Laguna you get this atmosphere because you're racing in front of all these fans and the world stage," Ben says. "There's a bit of extra adrenaline, for sure."

The Laguna victory gave Ben a 24-point lead, but the series was heading for six races at three of Mladin's strongest tracks—Mid-Ohio, Virginia International, and Road Atlanta. One thing could certainly be said about Ben's emergence in 2006: It had sparked Mladin and his crew to work harder than they ever had in their careers, and it was paying off. The Aussie sensation came storming back with six consecutive victories, in the process establishing a new record for AMA Superbike wins in a season. Fortunately for Ben, he was able to finish as runner-up in all of the races, but in spite of Ben's best efforts at Road Atlanta, Mladin took back the series lead by three points going into the season finale at Laguna Seca.

Looking back on the 2007 season, Ben says that even though he wasn't thrilled about finishing second to Mladin for six straight races, he was confident about the last race.

"Laguna had always been a good track for me, and not so great for Mat," Ben explains. "I had a really good feeling going into that last race. In racing you can never take anything for granted, because the sport is unpredictable, but I knew that if I didn't have problems and I rode [the way] I knew I could ride, it would be a good outcome."

The tension and anticipation was at an all-time high at the Laguna Seca finale. Ben set the tone early by winning the pole, and the championship point that went with it. It was a critical point, too. Had Mladin earned the pole it would have been possible for him to win the championship, even if he finished second to Ben.

As the riders lined up for the start of the deciding race, a thought came into Ben's mind: "Forty-five minutes left in the season. Give it 110 percent. Let's go."

The race was riveting, with Mladin pulling out to an early lead and Ben trailing right behind him. It went like that for most of the way, and then Ben made a slight mistake, allowing Mladin to stretch his lead to a full second. At that moment it appeared that Mladin's renewed focus would earn him the title over his archrival, but Ben immediately closed the gap, and with 11 laps to go the leaders came upon a lapped rider. "I saw the lapper coming," Ben remembers, "and I got right up kind of beside Mat, where he couldn't quite see me, and I was thinking if he was going to go for the lapper, I'd have no chance, but if he shut off a little early, then I could maybe get in that gap. I got in the gap, and then he came back by, and we struggled to stay on the track too. I didn't know if he ran off or not. It was just one of those close things. I'm sure it looked pretty cool on TV."

With the pass and now in the lead, Ben gradually pulled away to a five-second lead. Ben's last lap celebration allowed Mladin to get within 2.5 seconds at the finish line, but it didn't matter. Ben had pulled it off. He'd taken Mladin's best shot and come out on top in one of the all-time epic battles in AMA Superbike history.

Pulling into the pits the celebration began. Ben's crew and his family and friends were there to greet him. Mary gave Ben the gift that Lisa had bought him the day of his Daytona victory six months earlier. "They're awesome," Ben says of the diamond cufflinks.

"That championship was my favorite of the three AMA Superbike titles," Ben would later say. "Mat came back at me strong that year, and I just played it smart and pulled it out when I needed to. It really confirmed my feeling that you don't need to win every race, even though every bone in your body tells you to go for the win every time you're on the track."

Mladin was subdued in the post-race press conference. When asked if he still considered the season a success, he answered halfheartedly, "Oh yeah, sure. We gave up some points; if we were thinking about championships, as I've said to you guys before, we've given up points in a couple of races, just through riding hard and trying to get race wins. That was the plan at the start of the year. So to be disappointed now would be somewhat hypocritical, because we did what we wanted to do, and that was try and win as many races as possible. And we come up a point short in the end, and so what? Who cares? I'm happy, honestly. It's a great season. I thanked Ben on the podium for helping me become the racer that I am, because he's . . . I had to pick up my pace and pick up my game to get up to his level, and it's been a really good year. We're looking forward to the off-season. Go home and start working, do a few things different, and see if we can't come back for another shot at it next year."

Ben also won the AMA Superstock Championship that season. The extra bonus was great for his pocketbook, but winning that title really was anticlimactic. It was so lopsided; Ben won all but two races, and there was never any mystery as to who would win the title. It would be the last time Ben would race in a support series.

Off the track Ben's personal life provided much fodder for press speculation, perhaps fueled even more by the fact that Ben is intensely private about his life away from the paddock. In terms of relationships, Ben has had girlfriends but admits that his intense focus on racing makes relationships somewhat difficult.

"I don't think I'm unique in this, but as a racer I'm a bit selfish in some ways," Ben says. "I'm into my racing, and at this point it's number one to me. It's my job and it's my passion and it's all I think about, and something I dedicate a lot of time to. As a result, that hurts my personal life. At the same time I realize that I'll be done with racing when I'm 35, and I would like to find someone who could put up with me then.

"I'd rather have *a* girlfriend than juggle five girls and have the rock-star lifestyle. I'm definitely not like that."

In terms of close friendships, he and Jamie Hacking became training partners, and that grew into the two becoming close friends. They traveled to the races by motor coach, finding that life on the road was a lot more enjoyable if they caravanned and trained together between races.

"I picked up a lot of things from him," Ben says of Hacking. "He was always laughing at me for my habit of planning everything. Jamie was a little more spur-of-the-moment. He helped me learn to relax a little more. At the same time I think he picked up some things from me too. Jamie is the

kind of rider who felt like he should win every race, and he would be upset if he didn't. I think he saw how I handled things—that maybe you don't have to win every race; you just have to put in good rides every weekend to stay in the championship. That's kind of my mentality with a lot of things, not just racing, and I think Jamie picked up on that."

Ben and Jamie became almost like brothers. Each would watch the other on the track and give valuable input on what they noticed. Ben credits Jamie a lot for his Superbike championship-winning 2006 season.

"It wouldn't be so much that he'd give me pointers on my riding," Ben explains, "but he would watch other riders who were doing well at a certain point on the track and come back and tell me what they were doing. And sometimes when I was going into a panic, he'd remind me to keep it under control. We'd go to dinner together and were always winding each other down after the races."

It was Ben, several years later in World Superbike, who kept talking up Jamie, which was in large part the reason

Jamie got to ride as a fill-in rider with Kawasaki for three rounds when Makoto Tamada was injured in 2009. Ben said it was like he was able to return the favor for Hacking beating Mladin for second at Road America in 2007. "I won the championship by a single point that year, and Jamie beating Mat made the difference," Ben says.

Besides being helpful friends, Ben says that sometimes he and Jamie would just simply have fun together.

"I remember his trailer was always having [tire] blowouts," Ben recalls. "Once it happened outside El Paso, Texas. It blew out two tires. We jacked up the trailer, got the tires, and went into town to get them fixed. We left Rachel [Hacking, Jamie's wife] and my dad in the motor coach on the side of the interstate. While we were waiting for the tires to be repaired we went shopping at the mall, and I remember we came out of the mall and had shopping bags and vanilla Frappuccinos and I looked at him, thinking about my dad and Rachel getting blown around by wind gusts every time a semi came past, and said, 'If Rachel and my dad saw us right now, they would kill us.'"

Jamie says in spite of being the older of the two, it was Ben who normally kept the duo from going completely out of control. "Ben's a little more conservative than I am," Jamie says with a chuckle. "We'd be out fooling around and I would want to push the issue, and he'd be the one trying to pull things back.

"At some tracks in certain areas I was better than he was, and in others he was strong. We always tried to help each other to find out what we were doing to get through a tricky section.

"He really talked me up when he was at World Superbike, and even though it was Kawasaki in the U.S. that got me the World Superbike and MotoGP wild cards, it didn't hurt that I had Ben there in my corner," Jamie says.

Ben went on to win the 2008 championship over Mladin again, but the fire of the battle seemed mostly extinguished by that season's developments. One factor: The AMA, which had controlled professional racing in America since 1924, sold that role to the Daytona Motorsports Group, which was headed up by, Roger Edmondson, the former AMA roadracing manager. Edmondson had left the

AMA under bad terms back in the mid-1990s and had won a large settlement in a lawsuit against the association. Back in control again, it seemed that Edmondson was out to settle old scores, and DMG's relationship with the manufacturers seemed fractured from the start. This, combined with the sinking U.S. economy, meant that budgets were drying up. It was like the air was being let out of a balloon for America's motorcycle roadracing series. Instead of the focus being on the Spies/Mladin rivalry, the press was concentrating more on the rapidly diminishing series and the open disagreements between Mladin and Edmondson about how the series should be managed.

In spite of the fact that Spies vs. Mladin had produced the most intense rivalry in AMA Superbike racing since Wayne Rainey and Kevin Schwantz 20 years earlier, Edmondson publicly stated that he wouldn't cross the street to watch a race where only two riders could win. The implications

ABOVE: For the second year in a row, Ben held aloft the plate identifying him as the best in the U.S., this time while wearing a specially designed Alpinestars pullover. The championship came during the year that Mazda Raceway Laguna Seca was celebrating its 50th anniversary. (RILES & NELSON)

Ben hounds Mladin through the Corkscrew as the pair pulls away from Honda's Jake Zemke (top) in the first half of the race. Ben passed Mat on the 16th lap to take the win. With Mladin earning the extra point for leading two more laps than Ben, 15 to 13, he closed the points gap to 1. Had they tied in points, Mladin would have won the title by virtue of having more Superbike wins over the course of the season. (RILES & NELSON)

were clear: Edmondson thought Suzuki's Superbikes had a major advantage over the other manufacturers, and he intended to level the playing field. One *Cycle News* editorial by Henny Ray Abrams pointed out what was obvious to most: There was a very good chance that the reason Ben and Mladin were dominating racing was because they were the two most dedicated and talented riders the series had seen in years.

Under the new leadership the energy was quickly gone from the series. Mladin was disqualified from wins at Virginia International Raceway, and even though Ben had enough points on Mladin and would have won the title regardless of the disqualification, the perception was that the DMG was singling out Mladin for extra scrutiny because of his outspokenness.

"That whole season was a major mess," Ben said. "I won the championship, but it almost seemed like the focus wasn't on the race track with all the drama happening off the track."

The chaos meant that it was a good time for Ben to be looking for an escape route—one that would help him get a MotoGP ride as quickly as possible. In an effort to do so, Ben had hired an agent who had worked with John Hopkins in MotoGP, but after two years his efforts to secure a MotoGP ride for Ben remained unsuccessful. Certainly Ben had vastly superior credentials to get into the top level of motorcycle competition, but MotoGP, like the AMA, was contracting, and rides were few and difficult to get unless you brought major sponsorship dollars to the table.

In the end it was Keith McCarty, the longtime racing boss for Yamaha-USA, who was able to get the job done. He got Ben out of the AMA series and into World Superbike racing, along with Yamaha Motor Europe racing manager, Laurens Klein Koerkamp, who's based in Amsterdam.

Negotiations for 2009 were not going well with Suzuki. In spite of being on the verge of winning three straight AMA Superbike Championship crowns, Ben was concerned that American Suzuki's management (and primarily Mel Harris) seemed more committed to Mladin than to Ben. The Spies family had little doubt that the American Suzuki camp was divided, with Mel Harris backing Mladin and Mr. Itoh backing Ben. This was a source of frustration for Ben, but it also helped him with his decision to look elsewhere for a ride, especially when he received some critical encouragement from Mr. Itoh around midsummer 2008.

"We always felt like we treated Ben and Mat equally," said Yoshimura Suzuki's manager Don Sakakura. "I can understand, though, how Ben and his camp might feel [differently]. There was one specific instance I can think of where Mat was given preferential treatment because of a technical issue, and that was probably a mistake on our part, and Ben was upset by the circumstance."

Sakakura was referring to a race at Infineon in 2008 where Mladin's crew was allowed to change the front forks on his bike back to an earlier version, even though the team had established a relationship with a different suspension maker. Ben also wanted to go back to the previous fork setup, but was not permitted to do so.

"That was one where I had to really bite my tongue," said Tom Houseworth, who was torn between loyalty to his bosses at Yoshimura and being able to give Ben the setup he wanted on his Superbike. "I told Ben to just put it out of his mind and just go out there and prove a point, and he did. He won both races. This was a major statement that Ben could overcome something like that and not sulk about it. Instead, it made him even more determined to go out and win."

"I was a loyal guy," Ben explains. "I liked it at Suzuki. They were the company that took the chance on me. I liked riding for them, and also liked the idea of sticking with one manufacturer for my entire career. When they started showing me that Mat was a higher priority, it was tough. I would have probably stayed with Suzuki, wherever they wanted me to race, but it just seemed like, 'Oh yeah, you won three championships for us, but we're not that interested in keeping you.' I know how negotiations go, and I'm sure we were driving a hard bargain; it may have just been Suzuki's way of trying to soften us up when it came to contract time, but it didn't go over well, I can tell you that."

At Indianapolis in July of 2008 Ben tested the Rizla Suzuki MotoGP bike. With the opportunity to race as a wild card in MotoGP that season, Ben's focus began shifting from the domestic American series to his future in World Championship competition. (LARRY LAWRENCE)

CHAPTER 16 — WILDCARDS, CHAMPIONSHIPS, AND NEGOTIATIONS

Even though some within American Suzuki appeared to be giving the cold shoulder to Ben, it seemed that the parent company was committed to keeping their young talent. At the end of 2007 Ben got his first opportunity to test the Rizla Suzuki GSV-R800 as part of a factory MotoGP team test in Sepang, Malaysia. One test in Malaysia was particularly hard on Ben— not just because of jet lag and the sleep-deprivation problems his family is cursed with, but because a well-respected mentor was dying.

Although veteran crew chief Merlyn Plumlee never worked directly with Ben—he spent most of his career at Honda—he was universally admired in the paddock and always willing to share his immense knowledge with Ben, as he'd done when he worked with Nicky Hayden. Ben wrote his last e-mail to Plumlee and received one back shortly before Merlyn died after a two-year battle with lung cancer.

The test in Malaysia ended up being rained out—the second time this had happened—and it wasn't until the end of the MotoGP season that Ben finally got on Suzuki's 2007 MotoGP bike at Valencia. He was accompanied by mentor Kevin Schwantz on another GSV-R.

Ben's first MotoGP experience was a positive one. On a new track and a bike he'd never ridden before, Ben got within a second of the lap time that John Hopkins ran in the race, and even closer to the lap times of Rizla Suzuki's Chris Vermeulen—all of this in the span of just 33 laps.

- -

ABOVE: Ben is a huge dog lover. Here he spends some time with his dog Freedom, rescued from a pound when just a puppy. (LARRY LAWRENCE)

Tom Houseworth recalls that Ben had a big smile on his face when he pulled in the pits for the first time. "The Suzuki GP bike, with all its electronics, had a reputation for being tough to ride. You could tell Ben was relieved that the bike turned out not to be that difficult."

In fact, Ben found the GSV-R far from intimidating. "It seemed like an electric motor," he says. "The bottom-end power is not as torquey as the Suzuki Superbike I was used to, but overall it was pretty fast. The biggest difference was the tires didn't move around at all. Of course, I wasn't pushing it to the point where I had any grip issues. Even though it was a short session, I was happy to get some laps on the bike and get just a little experience that I could put in my memory bank."

In May of 2008 it was officially confirmed that Ben was going to be given two wild-card rides with Rizla Suzuki in the two American MotoGP rounds—Laguna Seca and Indianapolis. Indy was a complete nightmare, as his leathers and helmet failed to make the flight. "My mom had to stay on the phone all night long to secure the gear's arrival," Ben says. "She hounded that airline."

Behind-the-scenes negotiations were already under way to get Ben in MotoGP for 2009. The result was that these wild-card rides would be a tryout of sorts for Ben. That put a lot of pressure on him and set off the most intense and busy summer of racing he would ever experience. Not only was he trying to focus on winning a third AMA Superbike title, but now his future was standing in front of him, and with minimal experience he suddenly had to go out and prove he belonged at the World Championship level.

Some of that pressure was mitigated when Rizla Suzuki's Loris Capirossi was injured at Barcelona and Suzuki invited Ben to come over to race the British Grand Prix. It was the perfect no-pressure scenario for Ben. On a track he'd never seen and getting only his second taste of the Suzuki GP bike, Ben acquitted himself well in his MotoGP debut, qualifying 8th and then scoring World Championship points in his first ride with a 14th-place finish.

The results don't tell the full story. Donington Park has a notoriously tricky surface in the dry that is even more treacherous in the wet, which it was during qualifying. When

ABOVE: **Flames shoot from the exhaust of Ben's Yoshimura Suzuki Superbike during the AMA Superbike race at Barber Motorsports Park in April of 2008. Ben spent so many hours testing and racing the Suzuki GSX-R Superbikes that he said it felt like an extension of his body.** (LARRY LAWRENCE)

Ben skims the Auto Club Speedway grass with his knee and elbow while fending off Mladin in Saturday's Superbike race in 2008. Ben won both races in Fontana, then 5 more in a row to push his winning streak up to 7. He would win 3 more to end his AMA career with 28, good for third on the all-time list. (RILES & NELSON)

Ben and close friend Jamie Hacking (right) go after each other with champagne in Sunday's Superbike winner's circle at Infineon Raceway in the wine country north of San Francisco. Ben won both races that weekend, with Hacking finishing third on both Saturday and Sunday. (RILES & NELSON)

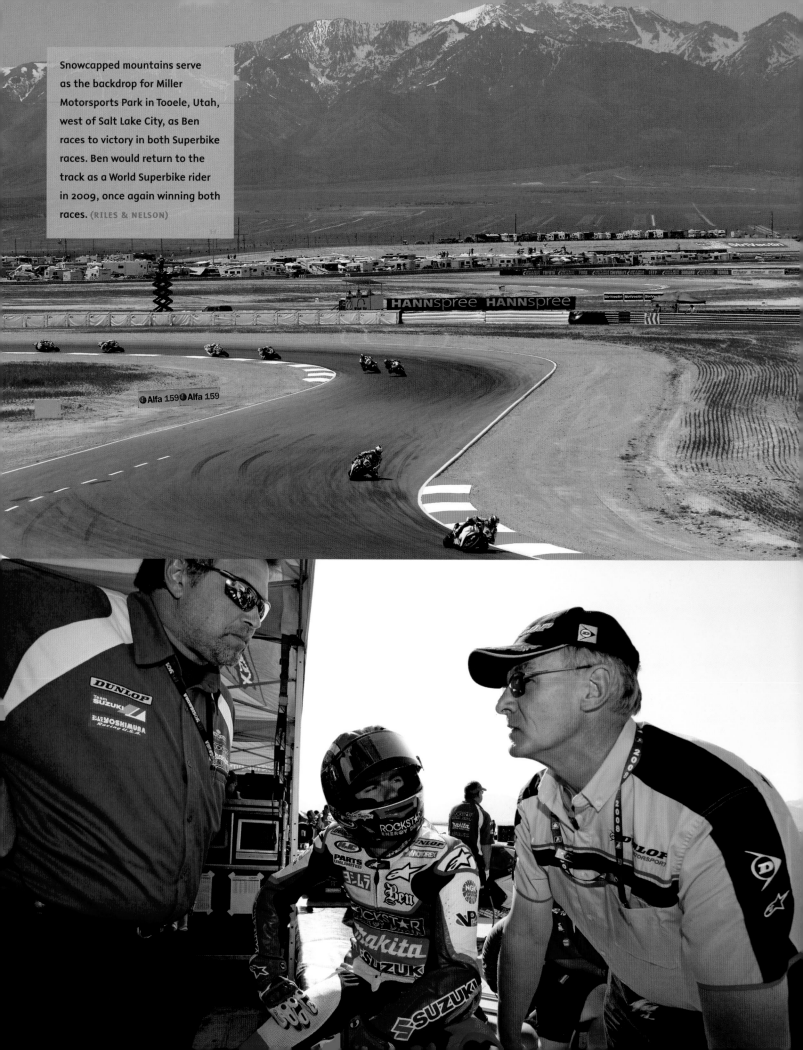

Snowcapped mountains serve as the backdrop for Miller Motorsports Park in Tooele, Utah, west of Salt Lake City, as Ben races to victory in both Superbike races. Ben would return to the track as a World Superbike rider in 2009, once again winning both races. (RILES & NELSON)

Ben qualified eighth, the riders behind him included Dani Pedrosa, Jorge Lorenzo, and John Hopkins. The hour in the rain denied the team valuable setup time, which would be crucial because the race was run on a dry track.

"It was frustrating because I started so slowly," Ben said after his GP debut. "The biggest difference was how the GP tires reacted compared to what I was used to with Superbikes. I was just flat-out slow those first eight laps or so. I wasn't happy with my results. The one thing I took away as a positive from the race was how I started to get a little more comfortable with the bike, tires, and everything late in the race. By then it was too late, but I could definitely see a learning curve there."

He said the breakthrough for him came about halfway through the race when he slid the rear tire for the first time. "Right then I felt I knew what the bike was going to do when I pushed it, and that gave me some confidence."

The main thing Ben said the British GP did for him was to give him seat time on the GSV-R before his wild-card rides in America.

Controversy sprang up the following week at Assen, during the Dutch TT. It was on Thursday afternoon, the first day of practice, when Capirossi crashed hard in his return to action. He suffered a bad puncture wound to his forearm and was just generally beat up, and announced he wouldn't be able to race that weekend.

Team manager Paul Denning, wanting to field two bikes, asked Ben at the last minute to fill in for Capirossi, but after talking it over with his manager at the time, his mother, and Kevin Schwantz, Ben decided it would be best not to take Denning up on the offer. Ben was surprised when, instead of respecting his choice and moving on, Denning talked to the media and expressed his dismay that Ben hadn't taken the offer to ride.

RIGHT: The team unloads Ben's bike after a rare qualifying crash at Road America in Elkhart Lake, Wisconsin, in 2008. Ben survived a front-end washout in the final corner of the high-speed, four-mile track to take his fourth pole in a row, up to that point. "Yeah, it was weird," Ben recalls. "It was one of those low-sides where I didn't have any warning." (RILES & NELSON)

Ben picks up the narrative. "The complete story is this: Paul [Denning] came to me at Donington and thanked me for doing the race, but told me I could now go on holiday or go home, as Loris wanted his bike back, and Paul had to abide by his rider's request. My mom said, 'You aren't going anywhere until you talk to Masayuki Itoh. Paul Denning may own that team, but he did not invite you personally. The invitation came from Japan Suzuki to American Suzuki for you.' Mr. Itoh confirmed that it would be an insult to quit the invitation extended to me, and said to go to Assen and view the race. However, he said if something happened I must have a practice before getting on the bike, as I had a responsibility to the championship chase I was in with Mladin in the USA.

"I went to Assen and in practice Loris went down, on Thursday afternoon. I waited for over 30 minutes, with gear, for Paul to call to me for help. The call never came. Then he comes to me and asks me to help him and to go qualify and race. [Ben would have had a one-hour practice on Friday morning before qualifying in the afternoon.] What a dream come true! I get another opportunity. My old management and Kevin Schwantz were like, 'You just have to do this. You couldn't let a break like this go.' My mom was pretty mad. She and I walked outside, and she told me that I knew the agreement; Kevin did not know it. I told her I wanted to talk to everyone in the hospitality lounge area and would make up my own mind. She was hot. She said, 'No, you will let a great dream and a bunch of people talk you into something. You know where your priorities lie.' I asked her to go out to

the parking lot and wait for me there because, like I say, she was hot mad. Anyway, I knew the deal with Japan and America, and I knew where I was sitting in the championship, and really, it would have been crazy to jeopardize all of it with no practice and not knowing the track.

"That one kinda didn't go over well," Ben says. "I mean, they'd already had a full day of practice, they wanted me to come in there on a track I didn't know, with everyone else already dialed in, and ride? There was no way I was going to come out looking good in that situation, and Denning knew that, yet he went to the press and made it sound like I was abandoning the team when they needed me, and it got played up in the press like that.

"Another thing was, I think, the way that was handled made it look like I wasn't a team player to Suzuki. And, I can't say for sure, but I think that was part of the intention of Denning—to sort of make me look bad. He could have just said that my decision not to race Assen was understandable, and left it at that.

"I knew I had the Indy test coming up, and that would give me a real chance to get to know the bike in a controlled situation. Here I was in the middle of looking for a ride for the next season, and the last thing I wanted to do was to get on the bike and circulate around in last place. That wasn't going to do me or the team any good." It was at this point that Ben began to realize his future probably wouldn't be with Suzuki's GP team.

A little known backstory to the mounting tension between the Spies camp and Rizla Suzuki was the fact that Ben's mentor, Kevin Schwantz, was openly lobbying Suzuki to run a MotoGP squad, and it was quite apparent that if Schwantz was able to get the support from the factory to field a team, that Ben would be his rider. Still very popular in the GP paddock, Schwantz was surprisingly open in his criticisms of Rizla Suzuki and the lack of results the team produced. At the same time the Spies camp was using whatever political capital they had within Suzuki, working behind the scenes as Schwantz's advocate in this attempt at either forming a new team or taking over Suzuki's MotoGP efforts. While he never said it publicly, it's easy to understand why Denning would be less than enthusiastic about this potential coup.

So it was, with this contentious setting serving as a backdrop, that Ben tested the Rizla Suzuki at the legendary Indianapolis Motor Speedway. He proved he was a team player at Indy. Ben went above and beyond the call of duty by turning 205 laps of practice in just two days, giving the team an invaluable amount of data going into the MotoGP debut at Indy.

During the close of the Indy test Ben had the fastest time of the session, turning a 1:43.091 when he left to catch a flight back to Dallas, with about an hour of track time remaining. Ducati test rider Niccolo Canepa went out in cooler conditions at the very end of the day and slightly improved on Ben's time, clocking a 1:43.006. Ben found out about it just as he was getting ready to board the plane to Dallas, and he was ticked, to say the least. Even though he'd turned in over 200 laps, he was upset at himself for not staying to the very end. "Man, I should have stayed one more night there in Indy and gone out and left that session with the best time," he says. "I was so exhausted from the

On the gas hard out of the final turn 11 at Laguna Seca in the first of his two wild-card rides on American soil. Ben acquitted himself well in the race; he was the second Suzuki, and finished eighth overall. (RILES & NELSON)

RIGHT: Ben instantly became one of the fan favorites as a wild-card entry at the Red Bull Indianapolis GP. Wherever Ben went in Indianapolis he was followed by a throng of enthusiastic fans. His popularity only grew when he became a World Championship regular. (LARRY LAWRENCE) **BELOW LEFT:** In his first grand prix as a wild card on American soil, Ben chases teammate Loris Capirossi (No. 65), while holding off Toni Elias (No. 24) and fellow Texan Colin Edwards (No. 5) at Mazda Raceway Laguna Seca. Ben finished 8th, narrowly losing 7th to Elias, while Edwards and Capirossi were 14th and 15th, respectively. (RILES & NELSON) **BELOW RIGHT:** MotoGP riders line up at the famous yard of bricks in advance of the inaugural Red Bull Indianapolis GP in 2008. Ben is standing almost exactly in the middle between Rizla Suzuki's Chris Vermeulen and then World Champion Valentino Rossi. (LARRY LAWRENCE)

RIGHT: The city of Indianapolis temporarily renamed some of the downtown streets for the MotoGP riders competing in the 2008 Red Bull Indianapolis GP. Ben stands on the street renamed for him. (LARRY LAWRENCE) **ABOVE:** Mladin gets sideways trying to pass Ben into turn four at Virginia International Raceway in 2008; this is typical of how the pair fought for three years. Mat won both races, but the AMA disqualified him for an illegal crankshaft and denied his appeal on the grounds that he hadn't filed the proper evidence to refute the AMA's findings. (RILES & NELSON)

two weeks in Europe and all the testing at Indy, that all I could think about was getting back home and resting."

Ben went home to Texas and collapsed from exhaustion. He was hoping a few days of doing nothing would bring him back to his normal self, but in the days leading up to the Red Bull U.S. Grand Prix at Laguna Seca, he could tell something was wrong. By now Ben was reaching a peak of fitness and training, getting as lean as possible for the GPs. After years of working with trainers, like any high-level athlete, Ben understood even the slightest detail of how his body was reacting under the stress of travel, racing, and training. Coming into Laguna he knew something was wrong.

"I was actually going backwards in my training," Ben explains. "At first I wrote it off to all the traveling I was doing, but my body wasn't responding to rest, wasn't recovering like it should. I was generally feeling weak and had the nagging suspicion that something was not right."

Ben was supremely confident about the GP at Laguna. He knew the track, and had plenty of testing under his belt on the Suzuki GP bike. Yet the weekend was going to be incredibly hectic, to say the least. It was a combined MotoGP / AMA Superbike event, and Ben would be doing double duty. By the race weekend it was all too clear to him and those around him that something was physically wrong with him. On a weekend that he should have been at his most enthusiastic and dialed-in, Ben instead was pale, listless, and feverish, wanting nothing more than to find the bed and pillow in his motor home.

He struggled through the Laguna weekend, under-performing in both the MotoGP and Superbike races. Ben finished eighth in the MotoGP race and second in the AMA Superbike round, but he'd gotten so dizzy after the GP race that he nearly didn't enter the Superbike event. "I mean, I'm battling my butt off to win the Superbike champion-ship and I am so sick at Laguna that I literally didn't care. I had to be helped off the bike after the Superbike race. You know how sometimes when you're driving late at night and are so tired you literally can't figure out how you got some-where? That's how I was in the Superbike race. I really didn't remember anything about the race. I was nearly delirious after the race. When I wasn't in bed, I was throwing up or sitting on the john." Driving to San Jose Airport he was in severe pain, and the plane ride to Dallas was even worse. He kept saying loudly, "I can't handle this pain anymore; get me to a hospital when we land."

When he got home to Texas he got worse and was rushed to the hospital. He went through a barrage of tests, and while doctors could not figure out definitively what was causing his problems, they did find that his body cavity was filling with toxic green fluid. He was in serious condition, much worse than the public knew. Had he not gone into the hospital when he did, he might have died from the infection. Doctors drained the fluid from him and performed an emergency appendectomy as a precaution, yet the problem persisted. The doctors never determined the exact source of Ben's illness.

Ben left the hospital and was prescribed powerful antibiotics. He began a slow and gradual recovery, but he'd lost seven pounds from his already-lean frame. He had a full schedule of races in front of him, yet he'd lost most of his fitness, and was too weak to train in order to get it back. The best he could hope for was that rest and the medicines he was given would help him turn the corner.

Ben raced the Mid-Ohio and Virginia International AMA Superbike rounds in a highly weakened state. Mid-Ohio was just one week after he was released from the hospital, and he had been told he could not sustain any injury to his abdomen or even brake hard in the car with the seat belt buckled. He nearly crashed at VIR when his bike got side-ways coming out of a turn and opened up the stitches from his recent surgery with a tank-slapper. Due to his stomach cavity still purging itself of toxins, his wounds were not heal-ing nearly as quickly as they normally would have. The near get-off at VIR actually tore his stomach muscles, something he didn't find out until visiting doctors the week after the race. Mladin took advantage to win both races at VIR.

In spite of all this, Ben was still in a strong position to win his third AMA Superbike title after one of the worst months of his life.

By the Road Atlanta round at the end of August Ben had turned the corner. While his fitness level was not back to what it had been before the stomach infection and muscle tear, he was at least feeling better, and able to eat and hold food down. He had started to get back on his bicycle and rebuild his energy, and it showed. In Atlanta Ben won the pole and came from behind to win Sunday's race. Surprisingly, it marked the first AMA Superbike win for Ben at Road Atlanta, a track he'd raced on since he was a 12-year-old amateur club racer.

Off the track Mladin had been disqualified from his VIR victories, making Ben the winner. It was found that Mladin's engine had an illegal crankshaft. There remained a great deal of speculation that Mladin was being punished by DMG for his criticism of the direction of the series. Teammates Ben and Tommy Hayden's motorcycles were not torn down as far as Mladin's, something the DMG even later admitted was a mistake. When an appeal by Mladin was denied, Ben clinched the championship.

"The thing that did bother me about the way 2008 ended was that people think that I was handed the championship when Mat lost his appeal," Ben said. "The thing was, I only needed to finish something like 19th or better at Laguna to clinch the championship even if he'd won the appeal and was given the points back from VIR. It wasn't the way I wanted to win that final Superbike title. It was bad for everyone, and it only confirmed to me how I needed to move on and race elsewhere."

With the Superbike championship decided, Ben shifted his focus to Indy and his final wild card for Rizla Suzuki. Ben qualified fifth at Indy and finished sixth in a torrential downpour brought on by the remnants of Hurricane Ike, the third-costliest hurricane ever to make landfall in the United States. What fans didn't realize about the shortened race was that Ben had ridden nearly blind the second half of the race when his face shield fogged up.

"It was insane," Ben recalls. "I literally could not see the apex of the turns or anything. I was trying to wipe off my visor while the bike was hydroplaning down the front straight at 150 miles per hour. Everyone was going through it, but the visor problem made it doubly hard. Considering all that, I was happy with my finish."

On September 28 at Laguna Seca Raceway in Monterey, California, Ben raced in his final AMA Superbike race. What should have been a major celebration instead felt like the relief of someone escaping a burning house. He had idolized the riders in AMA Superbike since he was a kid, and now he was only the fourth rider in history to win three straight championships, but the buddies he was leaving behind were going to go through some dark days as the series continued to free-fall under the new management and faltering American economy.

In a relatively short AMA Superbike career, Ben was able to place himself in the elite category of the championship. He placed in the top five in just about every category in the record books. He was the third-youngest rider to ever win the title, just behind Nicky Hayden and Fred Merkel. Ben was the youngest rider ever to reach the 20-win plateau in the series, third on the all-time AMA Superbike wins list, earned the longest winning streak ever, was second in all-time poles, and fourth in all-time winning percentage. The one stat that Ben blew everyone away in was podium percentage. In his four full seasons of AMA Superbike Ben amassed a mind-boggling 92 percent podium percentage rate. It was not simply the best in the history of AMA Superbike, but very likely by all research, also the highest podium percentage in the history of AMA professional racing.

Leading up to the Laguna AMA finale Ben already knew his future. He was heading to World Superbike with Yamaha. It was a surprise move. Most people were expecting Ben to land a GP ride, but with Suzuki giving him the cold shoulder, and the GP satellite teams that might have wanted Ben's services not able to afford them, the only realistic avenue for Ben was World Superbike.

Surprisingly, it was Yoshimura Suzuki's Don Sakakura who said he felt Ben made the right choice to sign with Yamaha.

"Given the direction Suzuki was going, Ben obviously had a great opportunity for World Superbike in a successful program. He proved his point quickly," Sakakura explains. "Looking back, it's hard to believe how quickly he progressed, winning the World Superbike Championship and then his instant competitiveness in MotoGP. We're proud to have been a part of Ben's career."

The 2008 Red Bull Indianapolis Grand Prix was shortened by 8 laps, from 28 to 20, when it was hit by Hurricane Ike. Ben finished a strong sixth, and only 1.5 seconds out of fourth, while running in a pack of MotoGP veterans for the entire race.

(RILES & NELSON)

The three Suzuki riders—Ben, Chris Vermeulen (center), and Loris Capirossi (right)—at the start of the 2008 Red Bull U.S. Grand Prix weekend. Vermeulen finished 3rd on the weekend, with Ben 8th and Capirossi 15th.

(RILES & NELSON)

uomini \ moto

Rider

ıtalıan magazın

La

SPECIALE STILE

// **VINTAGE**
// **OFF ROAD**
// **SURF**
// **MODS**
**Quando i Riders
fanno tendenza**

Becoming an instant sensation
in World Superbike made Ben an
international star in motorcycling.
He's especially popular in his second
home of Italy. Here he is featured in
the Italian magazine *Rider;* he was
also named 2009 Motorcyclist of
the Year by *Motorcyclist* magazine,
and was on the cover of the
program for the American round of
the World Superbike Championship.

(SPIES COLLECTION)

BEN SPIES
IL NUOVO FENOMENO DELLA SUPERBIKE

CHAPTER 17 — ON TO EUROPE

he move away from Suzuki—the factory that had gotten Ben as a teenage club racer and had helped to mold him into a multi-time national champion—was shocking. The Spies camp was looking at all the options on the table, but surprisingly, it was Ben himself who had first approached Yamaha about making the jump.

All of the catering to Mladin, and the special treatment and outright favoritism Ben believed Mladin was getting from Suzuki's Mel Harris, proved to be too much for Ben. "I had a lot of respect for a lot of people at Suzuki; don't get me wrong. I wasn't looking to be the guy that everyone was catering to," Ben says. "But I was just looking for a normal situation without all the drama. I wasn't enjoying racing. I'd go out for practice, qualifying, and the race, and then just go back to Jamie's [Hacking] motor home and hang out there. I didn't want to be around the team at all. It pissed me off because I liked the team, but I didn't like the environment. You'd walk in there and everybody was on eggshells."

Even after winning three championships, Ben felt the tension between himself and Mladin wasn't going to ease up. If Mladin was still going to be around, Ben knew he had to be on another team—if for no other reason than the fact he wanted to enjoy feeling like part of a team again, and not like an enemy in his own camp.

During a Superbike test at Road Atlanta in the middle of the season, Ben first made it known to Yamaha that he was looking to make a change.

"We were at the test and Halvy [Yamaha's roadracing team manager Tom Halverson] was coming down pit lane on his scooter, and I stopped him," Ben remembers.

ABOVE: Bicycling is a passion for Ben. He spends much of his off-season riding, and he even formed a professional cycling team. The hobby has made him one of the fittest racers in the MotoGP paddock. (LARRY LAWRENCE)

"I told him I needed McCarty's [Keith McCarty, the Yamaha factory race manager] number. He gave me the number quick. I talked to McCarty, and I told him I felt that I needed a change.

"And credit Keith, as we went down the road in negotiations with Yamaha, Keith badly wanted me to race in the AMA, but Japan wanted me to go to World Superbike, and Keith wanted to do what was best for the company overall."

Suzuki's Mel Harris admitted to Ben that he did not have any money to contract Ben, but was looking. Ben's budget from Japan had been spent elsewhere.

"I told them I knew I wasn't proven in MotoGP, but I thought I'd showed them I had good promise," Ben says. "I told them that I wasn't the kind of person that would be happy just being a GP rider; I had every intention of going over there and making an impact. But they were making every excuse not to even pay me what I was making in the AMA. I was going to be racing on the world level, with twice the weekends, maybe three times the commitments and all the travel, and they were making excuses."

The fact was that Ben was making more in AMA Superbike than many, if not most, of the MotoGP and certainly World Superbike riders, and he was finding it was going to be tough to earn a pay raise, even though he was moving up to the world level. Ben found it unbelievable that his mother could have done so well for him, yet no one else seemed able to match what she had produced.

With the Suzuki door closing, both Yamaha and World Superbike enthusiastically wanted the American champion to come and race, even to the point of the series organizers pitching in financially to make it possible. Infront Motor Sports, the company that runs World Superbike, pitched in by helping with Ben's living at the paddock with his motor coach. It was something the series hadn't done for other riders very often, but the promoters, desirous of having the American champion, made special accommodations.

While Ben really hoped to land in MotoGP, something he'd dreamed about since his childhood, a little taste of the World Superbike paddock turned Ben's feelings right around. From the very first tests at Portimao, Portugal, other riders were friendly to him, coming up and inviting him to dinner. The Infront people couldn't have been more accommodating, and they made Ben feel right at home.

"After years of so much conflict and drama, I couldn't believe how friendly, how family-oriented the World Su-

perbike paddock was," Ben says. "I remember there was a restaurant called Pino's at Phillip Island that everyone goes to after the race. Sunday night after I won my first World Superbike race, you would have thought I'd won the World Championship. I was with Andrew Pitt, and guys like [Troy] Corser, [Nori] Haga, and Yukio Kagayama were coming over to congratulate me. I had never felt that much welcome. It was just a good feeling, and it continued all year. It was so nice that I was sad to leave and go to GP, but for me, it's about learning and trying to get better and testing myself against the very best."

Yamaha was just introducing its new R1 in 2009, a motorcycle that featured a unique engine firing order that gave it potentially better acceleration, at the possible expense of outright top speed. However, Ben had many hurdles to jump during his first year in a World Championship series.

ABOVE: Yamaha road race manager Tom Halverson (left) and racing boss Keith McCarty (center), seen here talking to Ben Bostrom, were instrumental in helping get Ben on a Yamaha after a career spent on Suzukis. Ben first made contact during the season at an AMA test at Road Atlanta. McCarty wanted Ben to race AMA, but Yamaha had bigger plans. (HENNY RAY ABRAMS)

Not only was the bike new to him and the team, but he was also going to be racing tracks across the globe, nearly all of them for the first time, with a team of people he wasn't familiar with. Ben was also going through a major lifestyle change, making his European home in Cernobbio on Lake Como west of Milan, Italy, an easy drive to the team's shop in Gerno di Lesmo. It was a beautiful setting among the rich and famous, including new neighbors like George Clooney, but for Ben, it served more-practical purposes.

"The main reason I ended up there was because it was close to the team headquarters, and I wanted to spend as much time there as I could, so I could really get to be part of the team," Ben says. "And it was also perfect because the roads in that region were perfect for bicycling. A lot of elite cyclists live and train in the region, and I got to be friends with people in the cycling community."

Starting out as a way to simply get in shape, cycling had become a major part of Ben's life. In fact, if he weren't already a world-class motorcycle racer, one gets the distinct feeling that Ben would love to give professional cycling a try. One look at his physique and it's easy to see that Ben takes cycling very seriously. He transformed his body from a normal, standard-issue road racer's build to the form of a full-on pro cyclist: thin, but with a muscular upper body

and oversized quadriceps. His hard work in a bicycle saddle would pay off in motorcycle racing. Ben quickly became known as one of the best race finishers in the business, primarily due to his incredible fitness level.

"I feel like I have talent on a motorcycle, but so does everyone else on the grid," Ben says. "I think of my fitness as a secret weapon that can give me just a little bit of an edge when I need it."

When he entered World Superbike, Ben raced with Ryan Smith's number 19 as a tribute to his friend who had lost his life in a crash at Texas World Speedway. Despite the challenges of a new bike, new tires, a new series, and new tracks, Ben started 2009 with a bang by winning the pole for the season-opener at Phillip Island. As the season progressed, journalists noted Ben's almost freakish ability to learn tracks within a few laps, and then being able to win poles and set track records. Ben shrugged it off, saying,

"We get plenty of laps of practice before qualifying. If I can't learn a track in an hour or two of practice, I should be in another profession."

In spite of his modesty, as his rookie World Superbike season progressed, there was no denying that Ben had a special talent for rapid learning. Yamaha's ad agency even made light of his skill by producing a funny video showing Ben's supposed secret at learning tracks so quickly. It had to do with him visualizing the tracks as animals. The video became an Internet sensation.

One thing Ben did do that gave him some advance knowledge of tracks was play hours of racing videos. Some may discount that method of learning tracks, but fighter pilots spend many more hours in simulators than in actual flying situations, and the proof that Ben's technique worked was in his record-setting season of winning Superpoles.

In the Phillip Island opener Ben ran into trouble in the first race, being forced off the track twice—once to avoid a crash, and the other time, when a bike blew up in front of him while he was trying to charge back to the front. Ben rallied and outdueled Ducati's Nori Haga to win his first World Superbike race in his debut weekend. The pole and win in race two at Phillip Island gave Ben a lot of confidence.

"I knew at that point that I was at the very least going to be competitive in the series," Ben says. "Going into that first race I thought I'd be right there, based on what we'd done in testing, but you never really know until that first flag drops. I was also happy because I knew our bike was still early in development, and we were still able to turn consistently fast laps with it."

Ben had a perfect weekend in Qatar a few weeks later, taking the pole, winning both legs of the stop, and drawing to within 10 points of Haga for the lead in the championship.

Outside of the racing, the Qatar stop provided some humorous and crazy moments. At one point Ben was introduced to the Qatar crowd as American "spies," using the pronunciation for "secret agent." Then Mary inadvertently touched a sheik when trying to get his attention after he'd asked to meet Ben, to get a poster of him. Apparently that was a big no-no, and his entourage gave Mary a stare-down. Ben was so focused he hardly noticed all of these incidents. In spite of being on pins and needles the entire time in Qatar, Mary could later look back and laugh at the crazy things that happened.

Ben lost major ground to Haga in the championship at Valencia, where he did something he'd never done before in his Superbike racing career: He crashed out of a race. He minimized the damage by scoring second in the next race, but coming into Valencia he was just 10 points away from Haga. He left the Spanish circuit still in second, but 40 points down. Ben still had a positive attitude leaving Valencia. "I knew the Ducati would be strong here, and it proved to be true," he says. "We pick it up from here and go to Assen to try to get back on track and see if we can reset and get back to challenging for wins again."

Assen marked perhaps the highest and lowest points of Ben's World Superbike season. In the first race he made what many have described as one of the greatest closing-lap drives in series history. First, he and Leon Haslam ran side by side for three turns, with Ben taking back second—a pass that made the TV announcers go absolutely bonkers. With two laps to go, Ben was still nearly a half-second behind Haga, but he quickly narrowed the gap. On the final lap Ben made a daring inside move on Haga to take the lead, and then held his lines to edge the series leader by 0.154 seconds at the checkered flag.

Ben scarcely had time to celebrate one of his greatest wins before suffering a violent crash while leading in the second Assen race. The cameras captured Ben going off the

edge of the track and taking a spectacular tumble. "The bike felt very normal and I was able to get into the lead," he says. "On the second lap coming out of [turn] one, I just barely touched the edge of the track on the grass and had a big high-side. It was unfortunate, because I felt like I was riding well and the bike was great. I mean, I barely got the bike off the edge and that was the end of the race."

It was bitterly disappointing to Ben to realize that he'd crashed out of races twice in two weekends. It wasn't like him, and he's still at a loss to explain the sudden lapse. "Maybe it was a combination of still getting used to a new bike and tires, but I think more than anything it was [the fact that] I was pushing the limit every lap. I felt comfortable riding on the edge; maybe I got too comfortable or overconfident, but having those crashes taught me something that helped me become a better rider."

Unfortunately for Ben, Haga was the very picture of consistency and was beginning to really put some distance on him in the championship. Ben figured he would have to be perfect the rest of the year in order to have a chance at the title. What he didn't know was that the long World Superbike Championship had many extraordinary twists and turns still to come.

One of the first riders to befriend Ben in World Superbike was Nori Haga. This was before the two realized they would be locked in an epic battle for the championship. Nevertheless, the friendship continued throughout the season. Haga was now in his 10th full-time WSB season, and was one of the riders Ben looked up to when he was a kid racing mini-bikes. Haga was also a family man, married with two boys. Nori's five-year-old son Ryota took a liking to Ben. When the Hagas came to Ben's house in Italy for dinner, Ben played videos with little Ryota, and after that, Haga's son was always coming over to hang out with Ben at the races.

Even though he'd become a big fan of his buddy Ben, Ryota wasn't at all happy that "The Ben," as he called him, took what seemed like certain victory away from his dad in that first race at Assen. As the Hagas walked down pit lane past the Yamaha garage on the way to the podium after race one, Ben's mother Mary noticed that Ryota was crying

his eyes out. Mary asked him what was wrong. He looked up at her, obviously frustrated, and said, "My daddy is a loser, and I don't like The Ben!" With that, Ryota, still crying, quickly turned away from Mary and went to see his father.

Late that afternoon Ben was sitting alone in his motor coach, a little beat up physically from his second-race crash, but mainly upset with himself for letting his team down. Mary was letting Ben have some quiet time. She was answering text messages on her cell phone when she saw Ryota knocking on the coach door. He had some of his friends with him. Mary walked over and asked Ryota if she could help him. He said, "I want to see The Ben."

Mary said, "But I thought you didn't like Ben?"

"I *do* like The Ben, and he is hurt. I want to talk to him," Ryota demanded.

So Mary cracked the door open to ask Ben if he would see the kids. Ben, still smarting from his race crash, was trying to beg off from seeing the visitors when suddenly Ryota, perhaps taking after his dad, saw his opportunity. Before she could stop him, he'd edged his way past Mary through the slightly open door and run over to Ben.

"The Ben is hurt. Show me where you are hurt!" Ryota said with concern.

Soon the other children accompanying Ryota had flooded in and gathered around Ben. Ben sat up and started talking with them. One of the little girls in the group had a cast on her arm. Ben asked her what happened, and she said she'd fallen off a horse. When Ben told her she was brave for riding a horse, and that he was scared of horses, the little gang burst into laughter. So a friendship that was put to the test at Assen was restored by the end of the day. Even though Ryota likes it when his dad wins, little Haga still thought The Ben was at least the second-coolest rider in the paddock.

During the heart of the World Superbike season, Ben went to work, chipping away at Haga's lead. There were many highs and lows.

At Monza he had the first race won when his bike suddenly sputtered to a stop, out of fuel, on the final turn. The crew had made a mistake after a red flag and didn't get enough fuel in the tank on the gas-hungry circuit. Ben was nearly inconsolable after losing the race that way.

"I'd lost races before, but never by running out of gas on the last turn," Ben says. "I was so upset I just went to my motor home, got in bed, and buried my head under a pillow. I didn't know if I even wanted to come out for the second race. After working so hard to get back in the thing, I just knew the championship was lost on that mistake."

Ben won the second race and Haga crashed, meaning that in spite of running out of gas in the first leg at Monza, he left the historic circuit six points closer to series lead.

It was at Monza that the Spies camp began to realize that Ben's popularity was rising, especially with the rabid Italian fans. Ben had just been featured in several of the top magazines and newspapers in the country, and he was becoming a sensation. Ben was mobbed by fans so intensely as he tried to get around that the track had to issue security personnel just so he could get from his motor home to the paddock. Ben had never experienced that kind of adulation before, and he found it both exhilarating and a little intimidating.

"It really opened my eyes about how popular motorcycle racing is over there," Ben says. "In Texas I could go anywhere without a lot of people recognizing me. In Italy, everywhere I went I noticed people looking at me, nudging their friends. They were pretty good about giving me my privacy, though, and it was actually sort of fun to be a bit of a celebrity for the first time." Once Ben told the crowds that they needed to calm down—he hadn't even done anything yet!

In South Africa Ben struggled, his Yamaha down on power. He tried to make it up and had about the closest call of his career when he was thrown off his bike coming out of a turn. Somehow he landed back in the saddle and was able to continue. Originally it was thought that the impact of him landing hard on the bike had caused the shift linkage to fail in the second race, which resulted in another DNF. But in fact, the damage to the parts was done in Valencia, three races earlier. A communications breakdown was cited as the reason for the parts not being replaced.

Having mechanical issues that caused him to not be able to finish races was a new experience for Ben as well. In the AMA his Superbikes had never failed him. Ben and

Ben crashed in the first race in Valencia, Spain, in the third round of the championship. With Nori Haga taking a double win, Ben left Spain with a 40-point deficit after 3 of 14 rounds. (ANDREW WHEELER)

Despite being fierce rivals, Ben and Nori Haga struck up a lasting friendship during the 2009 season. Here Ben congratulates Haga after finishing second to him during the second race in Valencia. (ANDREW WHEELER)

The first race at Miller Motorsports Park was red-flagged on the sixth lap with Ben in the lead. When the race was restarted, Ben jumped right back into the lead and was already pulling away from Ryuichi Kiyonari (No. 9) as they went through "The Attitudes," a downhill sequence late in the lap at MMP. (RILES & NELSON)

The crowd at Miller Motorsports Park lets Ben know what they think after he completed the double with a win in race two. There was no question that most of the crowd who came to Utah came to see Ben win, and he didn't disappoint. (RILES & NELSON)

Houseworth decided they needed help. They brought in "Woody"—former Yoshimura Suzuki mechanic Greg Wood—to try to make sure every detail of the bike was covered. The addition worked perfectly. Ben's Yamaha was nearly flawless for the rest of the season.

Haga's Monza crash beat his body up pretty badly, and he struggled midseason just as Ben caught fire. Ben was dominant in the first race in Utah, winning by over nine seconds and dominating the second leg by a similar margin. It was an emotional victory.

"It was an amazing feeling to win an international event in your home country," Ben says. "I'd won plenty of AMA Superbike races in Utah, but to win a World Championship event with the home crowd cheering you on was definitely a special moment, and one I'm sure I'll remember for the rest of my life."

He also won Superpole for the seventh straight time, breaking the consecutive pole record established by fellow American Doug Polen in 1991. The weekend couldn't have been more perfect, and it certainly stood as a high-water mark in the season.

At Utah Ben took a major chunk out of Haga's lead, and at the halfway point in the season, Ben was 53 points down. Still a long way out, but certainly he'd take it after being 88 points down just one race earlier. Ben took 5 more points out of the lead at Misano, in spite of struggling with a bad front tire in the second race that caused him to struggle to ninth after winning the first leg.

It was another dominating performance for Ben in the British round at Donington Park. Two wins there brought him within 14 points of the series lead. At that round American Blake Young raced as a replacement for Suzuki's injured star, Max Neukirchner. Ben's success made the World Superbike teams revisit the idea of bringing American riders into the series. John Hopkins and Jake Zemke's fill-in rides were influenced in a major part by Ben's success. Young, who was pegged by American Suzuki to be the next Ben Spies, was also being mentored by Kevin Schwantz. Apparently someone in Young's camp had filled the young rider's head with unrealistic expectations about what he could do in Britain.

"Blake and I were sitting around talking, and he tells me that he can't wait, that he was going to be up there battling for the win," Ben says with a laugh. "I looked at him for a second and tried to figure out if he was joking. When I realized he wasn't, I leaned in and told him, 'Blake, whatever you do, don't repeat what you just told me to anyone else. You have no idea what you're stepping into here. These guys are fast, and they don't mess around.' Blake looked at me like I'd just popped his bubble or something." Young finished 25th and 17th in the two races at Donington.

Ben openly lobbied to get his buddy Jamie Hacking on a World Superbike. "I don't see anyone else who is getting podium finishes on a Kawasaki," Ben said about Hacking to anyone who would listen. So at Utah Hacking was given the opportunity to replace injured rider Makoto Tamada with Paul Bird Motorsport Kawasaki. Ben's faith in his friend seemed well-founded. Jamie rode the Kawasaki to an impressive 7th in the first race at Miller Motorsports Park but then ran off the track, took out Luca Scassa, and finished 19th in the second race, likely leaving the World Superbike bosses less than impressed.

Down the homestretch Ben continued to close the gap. At the race in Brno, in the Czech Republic, Haga's hard-charging Ducati teammate Michel Fabrizio got overexuberant and took out Ben in the first race. Ben bounced back and ended the weekend on a high note, winning the second race and closing the gap to just seven points. At the Nürburgring in Germany Ben actually took over the series lead, with a 1-2 finish. The first race in Germany was an instant classic. Haga led early with Ben in third. Ben passed Jonathan Rea for second, and on lap 11 of 20, Ben tucked into Haga's draft and outbraked him going into the Esses to take over the lead. Haga kept the pressure on and the duo ran wheel to wheel, until, with two laps to go, Ben made a strong surge to pull away and win by 3.85 seconds. Haga crashed in the second race with Ben taking second. That put Ben up by 18 points leaving Germany. "Things were looking really good at that point," Ben remembers.

Then at Imola Ben had an off weekend due to an electronic issue with his bike. He finished fourth and fifth, while Haga had a 1-2 and regained the lead. It was then one step forward, two steps back for Ben at Magny-Cours in France. Haga chased down and passed Ben late in the first race at Magny-Cours, but Ben remained calm and turned in a strong last half-lap, regained the lead, and held off Haga by 0.181 seconds in one of the most exciting finishes of the season. Ben ran well early in the second race, but with a front tire problem, he quickly fell back from the leading trio of Nori Haga, Max Biaggi, and Jonathan Rea. In the end Ben was 18 seconds behind Haga, losing the series lead and falling behind by 10 points.

Ben was philosophical about losing ground to Haga in the penultimate round. "Realistically, even if I'd won race two, Nori would have been close enough in the points that I still would have had to win at Portimao," Ben reasons. "So nothing changed. We had to put together a perfect weekend in Portugal. It was still possible to win the championship, and just to be in that position is a great feeling. Regardless of how it turned out, I felt like I'd had a phenomenal season."

Ben says the tension leading up to the final race at Portimao in Portugal was intense. "I could hardly sleep; some of the races earlier in the season just kept playing in my mind."

Surprisingly, when Ben actually arrived at Portimao and the race weekend got under way, he says a soothing calm came over him. "I don't know why," Ben says. "I just had in my mind that it was a simple equation: I needed to win both races, and having that single focus helped me concentrate on the task I had in front of me."

In the first race everything was going according to plan for Ben, when on lap seven Haga crashed. "It was actually a really tough race," Ben remembers of race one. "At first I was just going for the win, getting to the front and not worrying about anything. Then when Haga was out, I had to win, to get as many points as possible for race two. Once you have a gap, you don't want to be stupid and throw it all away."

Haga scoring no points in the first leg gave Ben a 15-point lead going into the final race of the year. In the second Portimao race, Ben ran as high as second early on, before gradually dropping back to a safe position at the tail end of the leading group of six riders. Italian Michel Fabrizio took the win in the second race, followed by Haga and Jonathan Rea of Great Britain. Ben passed Max Biaggi in the closing laps and cruised home to fifth. That finish was good enough to secure the championship for Ben by six points (462–456) over Haga.

Ben had done it. As a rookie he'd come back from a massive points deficit, raced on a new bike with a new team, on new tires and tracks, and won the World Superbike Championship. It will go down as one of the most impressive campaigns in the championship's history. Ben won the title with 14 race wins in 28 starts, and a record-breaking 11 pole positions. In a single season of racing Ben tied for 12th on the all-time World Superbike career wins list, and became the first American rider since fellow Texan Colin Edwards in 2002 to win the World Superbike title.

It could not have been a better scenario for Yamaha as well. That same weekend Yamaha secured the MotoGP title with Valentino Rossi, in addition to World Superbike and World Supersport titles on the same day. Ben's win gave

In his MotoGP debut for the Yamaha team, Ben finished seventh amid a five-rider pack contesting fourth place at the final race of the 2009 season in Valencia, Spain. Honda's Andrea Dovizioso (No. 4) was eighth. A year later, as a member of the Monster Yamaha Tech 3 team, Ben finished fourth. (ANDREW WHEELER)

Yamaha its first title in World Superbike and gave its new R1 motorcycle the perfect debut.

Ben's Yamaha World Superbike teammate, Tom Sykes, put Ben's accomplishments in perspective. "I think Ben having trusted crew in Tom Houseworth and 'Woody' [Greg Wood] at his side was a big benefit," Sykes says. "They seemed to work really well together. The only friction on the team may have come between Ben and Cal [Crutchlow, the Yamaha's Supersport rider who won the 2009 title]. I think there were some statements made by Cal that what Ben was doing wasn't special—that he could have done better. That obviously upset Ben.

"It was kind of sweet for Ben [when Crutchlow took over Ben's Yamaha World Superbike seat in 2010] that his results weren't duplicated; in fact, they were far from it. Unfortunately, I was being compared to Ben in 2009, and I think that the 2010 season proved, too, that maybe I wasn't doing such a bad job. I felt that if I had my own team behind me, like Ben—I'm not saying I would have challenged Ben, but I strongly believe I'd have been a lot closer."

"Valencia for me was the first step for 2010," Ben explains. "When I knew we were going to be racing MotoGP, I asked Yamaha if there was a possibility of racing as a wild card. For me, the whole reason was to get more time on the bike—it was basically three more days of testing. With the limited testing time, I felt it was important."

In his first race on the Yamaha MotoGP bike, Ben did quite well, finishing an impressive seventh in front of 94,000 fans at the Valencia Circuit. Ben's late-race pass on Andrea Dovizioso not only gave Ben his best dry MotoGP finish, but it also helped fellow Texan and future teammate, Colin Edwards, nail down fifth in the final MotoGP standings. "I told him I'd take him out and buy him anything he wanted," Edwards joked about Ben after earning a considerable bonus for finishing in the top five.

So 2009 ended as a major success for Ben: He'd won his first World Championship, gotten acquainted with the new Yamaha he'd be riding, and was gearing up for another rookie campaign, this time in the biggest show in all of motorcycle racing—MotoGP.

Ben is surrounded by the tools of the trade during the traditional debrief that took place following Saturday-afternoon qualifying at Mazda Raceway Laguna Seca in 2009. The image of pole-sitter Jorge Lorenzo (Fiat Yamaha) is on the top monitor, while Ben's fifth-place qualifying effort shows on the lower screen. (RILES & NELSON)

CHAPTER 18 — THE MOTOGP DREAM

The decision to move to MotoGP in 2010 wasn't an easy one. When Ben signed a two-year deal with Yamaha, he had the option to stay in World Superbike or to move to MotoGP the second year. He was invited to lunch after the WSB Monza race weekend, where it was made clear that Yamaha Japan, Yamaha Italy, and Yamaha Netherlands, the company's European headquarters, were very interested to hear what Ben wanted. As he took a deep breath and spoke, forks suspended in midair.

Months later he dropped by Mary's house and signed the contract to stay with WSB. Then he left for lunch. As his mother was driving to FedEx the contract, Ben called. Mary recalls that he said, "Wait! We need to talk."

"I knew I was going to MotoGP, be it in 2010 or '11," Ben says. "I enjoyed World Superbike so much, loved the people and everything involved with the series, but the more I thought about it, the more I realized that MotoGP was where I really wanted to be. I wanted to race at the highest level with the best riders on the ultimate machinery.

"I called Lin Jarvis [Yamaha's MotoGP team principal] back and told him I'd changed my mind and wanted to go to MotoGP, and thankfully he had enough faith in me to

- -

ABOVE: Ben and his dad, Henry Spies. In his early years Henry was a bit apprehensive about Ben's racing career, but once he realized how passionate his son was about the sport, he became a big supporter. Henry can often be seen at races around the world, rooting on his son. (LARRY LAWRENCE)

make it happen," Ben recalls. "Mom turned the car around with the dead-in-the-water contract for WSB." It didn't hurt that Monster Energy Yamaha Tech 3 owner Herve Poncharal had made it clear midway through the 2009 season that he wanted Ben on his team. Poncharal jumped at the opportunity to have Ben on his bike a year earlier than expected.

"I met Ben before when we were at Laguna Seca and he was racing in the support races," says Poncharal. "I had a strong interest in having him in 2009, but Yamaha wanted to keep our team as it was, with Colin [Edwards] and James [Toseland]. I was already a fan of Ben's before he went to World Superbike.

"I told Ben before he went to World Superbike to try to join the Yamaha family. For sure after he won a few races in World Superbike, I began talking with Yamaha and telling them of my desire to have him on my team. Some told me riders coming from 250 Grand Prix would be stronger, but I was convinced that Ben would be competitive in MotoGP, even in his first year."

When it was confirmed that Ben would be moving to MotoGP, Yamaha's Jarvis issued a simple statement:

Following the announcement of Ben's two-year deal with Yamaha one month ago, he has reassessed his options and decided that he would like to move to MotoGP sooner rather than later. Yamaha has considered his request, and together with Tech 3, we were able to find a way to make it happen.

Ben made sure he had some continuity in his move to MotoGP by stipulating that Houseworth and Woody would be part of the package. "I can't see why you'd want to break up a winning combination," Ben says. "Our results together spoke for themselves. Even in World Superbike we got off to a bit of a shaky start, but we rallied, and they had pretty much everything figured out by midseason. That was the kind of support I needed as I went to race at the highest level."

Houseworth says that making the moves from Suzuki to Yamaha World Superbike and then to Tech 3 Yamaha was a bit like changing schools.

"You get to a place where you know everyone, know what to expect, then all of a sudden you're in a new environment, and now, instead of having to face one Mladin, Ben's facing 10 of them," Houseworth explains. "We looked at coming to World Superbike as a challenge: new countries, new languages, new motorcycles, and new teammates. And then we come to MotoGP and it starts again. Just the logistics of traveling the world and making sure you have your visas and travel plans in order; people don't realize how big a task that alone can be. So moving to the world level has been a major challenge for everyone involved, and I think for the most part we've come out pretty well."

Ben stepped right into his new role as a grand prix rider with the experience of a veteran. His wild-card and replacement rides with Suzuki in 2008 and his decision to ride the final MotoGP of '09 paid off handsomely. Ben was solid in his first test with Monster Energy Tech 3 in Malaysia, doing a long race distance session to really get the feel of the Bridgestone tires in racing conditions. Ben was outstanding in the night tests at Qatar, turning the third-fastest time of the test. Already the expectations for the MotoGP rookie were growing.

Fresh off his World Superbike championship and now instantly competitive on a MotoGP bike, Ben was constantly hit with the question of comparing the Yamaha YZF-R1 Superbike to the YZR-M1 MotoGP machine. At first he found it difficult to articulate the differences, but as he got more experience on the GP bike, he was able to clarify one difference between the two types of racing machines.

"I found that with the GP bike you had to be really precise to go fast," Ben explains. "I had to change my riding style to suit the GP bike. You really have to trust the front end of the GP bike because your entry speed is so much greater.

"With the Superbike it seemed the harder I rode it, the faster I would go. If you needed to pass someone you'd just brake later and get on the gas earlier. With the GP bike it's not that simple. Everyone is so good on these bikes that passes are much more of a strategic thing that you have to really build up to and plan more carefully. Also, with the GP bikes having so much in the way of electronic controls, it

The mood is light on the grid late in the night at the Losail Circuit in Qatar as Ben prepares to make his debut with the Monster Yamaha Tech 3 team in the first race of the 2010 season. Ben finished fifth under the desert lights, and only 3.9 seconds behind the race winner. (ANDREW WHEELER)

The three amigos, Colin Edwards (left), Nicky Hayden (center), and Ben Spies, pose for photos at the end of the Thursday-afternoon pre-race press conference for the 2009 Red Bull U.S. Grand Prix. The Americans would finish together on Sunday afternoon, with Hayden fifth, Spies sixth, and Edwards seventh. (RILES & NELSON)

Mary Spies watches qualifying for the Red Bull U.S. Grand Prix with the rest of the team in the Monster Yamaha Tech 3 garage. Ben qualified fifth and would finish Sunday's grand prix sixth. (RILES & NELSON)

The elevation changes of the Corkscrew allow Ben to highlight his riding style during Friday practice for the Red Bull U.S. Grand Prix in Monterey. Ben finished Friday's two practices in fifth position overall, a performance he would match during Saturday qualifying. (RILES & NELSON)

seems that if you do make a mistake and fall off the pace, it's much harder to make up time. So your concentration level has to be incredibly high the entire time if you're going to have any hope of doing well in a MotoGP race."

Ben and Colin Edwards were a rarity as two Americans on a MotoGP team. Leading up to the season Ben was having a great time, really getting to know his teammate better. It was a unique relationship because Edwards was one of the riders Ben would go to watch race when he was growing up in Texas. They'd been friends for years. So it was a welcome experience for Ben to have a teammate he looked up to and could work with; more than that, they simply enjoyed each other's company.

Yamaha capitalized on their relationship by producing a video featuring Ben and Colin going on a vacation together, something Colin called a "mancation" in the hilarious short. The promotional video perfectly captured the Odd Couple personalities of both riders, with Colin playing the part of the outgoing, energetic, always-looking-for-fun type of guy, while Ben showed his actual traits of being more reserved and skeptical, and more easily embarrassed than his outlandish teammate. Having Edwards as a teammate was a far cry and a pleasant change from his days of being under the same tent with Mladin.

The first full season of MotoGP opened well enough for Ben. He went from 11th on the grid to finish 5th in the season-opener at Qatar. He then suffered bad outings at Jerez and Le Mans, retiring from the race in Spain with tire issues and then crashing out in France. Ben rebounded with a 7th in the Italian Grand Prix before really coming into his own as the season progressed, starting with his first—and somewhat unexpected—MotoGP podium finish at Silverstone.

"The Silverstone weekend was a bit odd because Colin and I both were the slowest bikes out there early in the weekend," Ben remembers. The race for the podium came down to a last lap battle with Nicky Hayden. "That last lap with Nicky was difficult to pass. I got a good drive onto the back straight and tried to pass him at Stowe Corner, but he came back by. On the next straight I managed to get by him and then had to ride defensively on the last part of

the lap. I was on the edge, but I had to go for the podium, and it worked out. I honestly didn't expect to get my first podium so quickly."

That third at the British Grand Prix meant that Ben had met one of his major goals just five races into the season. Ben proved his third at Silverstone was no fluke. He scored a fourth the following round at Assen, helping to erase the memories he had of his crash there the year before.

Before Laguna Seca, Ben and Colin—along with former World Champions Eddie Lawson, Kenny Roberts, and Wayne Rainey—were guests of American comedian and TV personality Jay Leno. Leno is a huge motorcycle racing fan, as well as a major collector of motorcycles and cars, and he hosted Yamaha's racing greats at his garage. It was a brush with Hollywood celebrity for Ben.

Interestingly, an American TV network had approached Ben and his management about doing a reality show based on his exploits in MotoGP and his life of the track. Mary was taken aback when the producers who'd approached them about the TV project later told her that Ben was too squeaky-clean for the project. They were looking for someone who had more "controversy" in his life. "I guess if Ben was a serious partyer, chasing girls every night, they might have done the show with him," Mary says, laughing.

Laguna didn't go as well as Ben had hoped. He was shooting for another podium at one of his favorite tracks, but after running as high as third, he battled past Hayden and was ready to try to get past Valentino Rossi late in the race when his helmet visor opened and distracted him, and he ran off the track. He had to settle for sixth. "Laguna was tough because I knew I should have run higher than I did," Ben admits. "Sometimes things happen that are out of your control."

Ben bounced back from the Laguna disappointment to earn his first MotoGP front-row start at Brno. It was a track that Ben had won on in World Superbike, and that helped, as he very nearly scored the pole. He held the number-one position in qualifying before Dani Pedrosa dug deep very late in the session to push Ben back to second starting position.

Ben was bugged a bit by the European media; it looked like they were downplaying his Brno accomplishment by speculating that since he was heading to the factory team the following year, Yamaha had already begun giving him factory parts. "The only thing we had on our bike was some updated electronics that we had at Laguna," Ben says. In the race Ben ran in the front group with Jorge Lorenzo, Dani Pedrosa, and Casey Stoner but fell back to his final position of fourth when his front tire went off.

Next up was Indianapolis, the site of Ben's first MotoGP two years earlier. It was one of the races that Ben thought he might win.

In the pre-race media blitz Ben got a chance to shoot a little basketball at Conseco Fieldhouse, home of the NBA's Indiana Pacers. Hosting Ben and the other riders at the event was former NBA All-Star Rik Smits. A native of the Netherlands, Smits is a longtime racing fan, and at the function it looked like he was as pleased to meet the GP riders as they were to meet him. The media on hand were impressed by Ben's basketball skills. At one point he sank three NBA three-point shots in a row to the cheers of onlookers.

The weekend at the world-famous Indianapolis Motor Speedway went about as perfectly for Ben as he could have dreamed. On Saturday he scored his first MotoGP pole, getting a standing ovation from the American fans on his cooldown lap. Ben's lap of 1:40.105 made the Texan two-tenths of a second faster than series leader and Indy's defending winner, Jorge Lorenzo. "Winning the pole in front of the home crowd was one of the proudest moments of my racing career," Ben recalls. The pole capped a special weekend that saw Ben confirmed in a press conference as a factory Yamaha rider for 2011. "I guess that was sort of the worst-kept secret in the paddock," Ben joked during the announcement.

In the race Ben again earned cheers from most of the enthusiastic 63,000 fans when he led the first six laps. Ben pushed his lead to as high as a full second, but 112-pound Dani Pedrosa and his Honda were a lightning-fast combination on Indy's long front straightaway. Ben held Pedrosa off for as long as he could, but with Dani's four-mile-per-hour top speed advantage, it was only a matter of time. On lap seven Pedrosa flew past Ben on the front straight. "I wondered if they put nitrous in Dani's bike, he came by me so fast," Ben joked. "When he passed me I knew I couldn't follow him, so I let him go and concentrated on keeping a gap to Jorge in third."

Being passed by Pedrosa didn't diminish the fact that Ben finished ahead of factory riders Jorge Lorenzo and Valentino Rossi. "I couldn't complain because it was a great weekend, and to be top Yamaha rider when you look at who else was on that bike, it was pretty satisfying. It took a while [for it] to sink in that I finished second in my home race, and [this] was definitely the highlight of the season."

From Indy Ben continued racking up solid finishes. In the final seven rounds he scored four top-five finishes. The only hiccup in the closing stages of the season was a crash on the sighting lap at Estoril, Portugal, that dislocated his left ankle. During the preceding round Ben had reached yet another milestone when he was awarded the coveted MotoGP Rookie of the Year Award.

"Ben's amazing season just gets better and better," team manager Hervé Poncharal said when Ben won the award. "To win the Rookie of the Year title with two races to go is a fantastic achievement for him and all of his Monster Yamaha Tech 3 crew. A lot of very talented riders came from the 250cc class into MotoGP this year, and they knew all the tracks, which Ben didn't. He's done a magnificent job, and done it with another impressive top-five finish. [Marco] Simoncelli never gave up, but Ben was too strong for him, and showed how strong he is on used tires."

Ben concluded the 2010 campaign with an excellent result in the season finale at Valencia, battling with Andrea Dovizioso and Marco Simoncelli to finish fourth in an exhilarating encounter.

Poncharal extended both his congratulations and gratitude to Ben afterwards, stating, "There is not much else I can say about Ben, because once again today he showed what an incredible talent he is. Sixth in the Championship is deserved for him and is an amazing achievement for a rookie, and I take great pride in knowing the Monster Yamaha Tech 3 Team played a big part in his success. I'd like to thank Ben for everything he has done for Tech 3, Yamaha,

RIGHT: Ben has his "race face" on during Friday practice for the Red Bull Indianapolis Grand Prix. Ben finished Friday's combined practice sessions sixth overall, then leapt to the pole position in Saturday qualifying. (RILES & NELSON) **BELOW LEFT:** Always willing to accommodate autograph requests, Ben signs one of the more-unusual items at Mazda Raceway Laguna Seca—a dog sweater. (RILES & NELSON) **BELOW RIGHT:** The Red Bull Indianapolis Grand Prix marked a milestone in Ben's young MotoGP career when he took the pole position in only the 11th race of his first full season. Here Ben takes one of the 2.62-mile track's 10 left-hand corners en route to out-qualifying Jorge Lorenzo (Fiat Yamaha) and Nicky Hayden (Ducati). (RILES & NELSON)

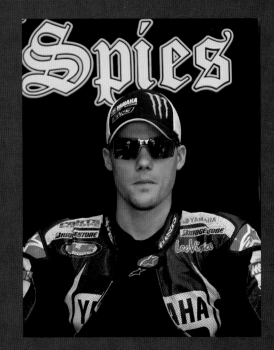

RIGHT: The second time through the Corkscrew sees Ben leading Andrea Dovizioso (Honda), Valentino Rossi (Fiat Yamaha), and Nicky Hayden (Ducati). Just ahead was Jorge Lorenzo (Fiat Yamaha), who would win the race from Casey Stoner (Ducati), with Rossi finishing third. (RILES & NELSON) **ABOVE:** Henry Spies (left) and crew chief Tom Houseworth keep an eye on qualifying at Mazda Raceway Laguna Seca. Ben qualified fifth for the race and finished sixth. (RILES & NELSON)

Ben leads the first lap of the Red Bull Indianapolis Grand Prix in front of Honda's Dani Pedrosa. Pedrosa passed Ben on the seventh of 28 laps and went on to win by 3.575 seconds. Ben had about the same gap on Fiat Yamaha's Jorge Lorenzo in third.
(RILES & NELSON)

Monster Yamaha Tech 3 team owner Herve Poncharal (right) gives Ben a big hug after he finished second in the Red Bull Indianapolis Grand Prix at Indianapolis Motor Speedway. The podium was the second for Ben in a rookie season in which he'd finish sixth overall and be the top non-factory rider.
(ANDREW WHEELER)

and Monster in 2010. I have no doubt he has a very bright future ahead of him, and it is a shame our experience together was so short. It was a privilege to have Ben on our team, and we will never forget his achievements. I wish him all the best for the future."

Ben was also proud of the fact that he finished as the top American in MotoGP, edging out his friend Nicky Hayden for the honor.

The fact that a Yamaha factory seat opened up, giving Ben the opportunity to step in was a major story of the 2010 season. The relationship between Yamaha's loaded stable of Valentino Rossi and Jorge Lorenzo was becoming ever more fractious. In fact, Rossi made it clear to Yamaha that there was not room for both on the team, leaving Yamaha in an uncomfortable position. Rossi was the king of the paddock, but clearly most believed that Lorenzo was the rider of the future. When Rossi was injured and Lorenzo dominated the 2010 MotoGP season, it became clear that Yamaha wasn't going to let the expectant World Champion go, so Rossi started looking elsewhere, and Ducati was more than thrilled to secure the services of the nine-time World Champion.

Ben was stepping into a new dynamic where he would clearly be the second rider on the team, but he was ready to accept that position.

"I'm coming in as teammate to the World Champion," Ben said. "It's not new for me. I've been in that position before, and that's fine. I still believe that if I go out and do my job, give my best in preparation, that my results will still be there regardless of my ranking on the team."

The 2011 campaign began immediately after the final round of 2010, when the teams tested at Valencia. Ben kicked off his first factory MotoGP ride on an updated Yamaha M1 by clocking in with the third-fastest time of the test, behind Honda-mounted Casey Stoner and new MotoGP World Champion Jorge Lorenzo. It was an impressive factory Yamaha team debut for the former AMA and WSBK champion.

"Not a big, big difference, but in every way the bike is better, which at the end of the day is big," Ben says, comparing the factory M1 with the Tech 3 satellite bike. "There's not one thing that I'd say is much better, just little things. Like the chassis and how it has more grip in places. It makes the overall lap time better. Also, being on the factory team helps. Just in terms of engineers and people looking at your data and maybe finding stuff that you didn't think was wrong."

Asked to judge what sort of performance would satisfy him in 2011, Ben says, "It's too early to speculate on what I can do. But as a rider, I want to improve in every way. I want to fight for the top five. I want to win a grand prix."

In 20 years Ben had gone from being a little guy on a mini-bike, riding circles in a school parking lot after-hours, trying to drag his knee like his heroes, to becoming a national and World Champion, and one of the elite riders in motorcycle roadracing. He is still a young man with many dreams to fulfill. He turns to the future in hopes of fulfilling his ultimate dream of one day becoming MotoGP World Champion. Whether or not he attains that lofty goal, one thing is certain: He'll have racing fans across the world rooting for him on his journey.

At round five in the 2011 MotoGP World Championship, at Catalunya, Spain, Ben celebrates a podium finish behind winner Casey Stoner and teammate Jorge Lorenzo. (ANDREW WHEELER)

ACKNOWLEDGMENTS

First and foremost, I thank Ben Spies and Mary Spies for giving me hours of interviews, both in person and via phone and Skype, as well as answering questions in countless text messages and emails. Ben's sister, Lisa, and father, Henry, were also generous with their time. Ben's good friends provided so much personal insight: Jeff Lemons, Ryan Landers, Randy Kienast, Jamie Hacking, and Jason Pridmore. Johnny Hodgkiss and Billy Wiese, Ben's former mechanics, told me much about the early days. Kevin Schwantz helped me understand the tremendous learning curve that Ben experienced as a young rider. Keith Cherry, who initially got Ben into motorcycling, made invaluable contributions. Don Sakakura and Herve Poncharal described what it was like to run a race team with Ben as their rider. Stuart Shenton, who guided Kevin Schwantz to a world championship, explained Ben's great testing savvy. Jeff Wilson recognized young Ben's talent and provided good stories from those days. Jim DiSalvo and Earl Hayden revealed the funny things that Ben did with their sons while growing up in the racing

paddock. Tom Sykes, Ben's World Superbike teammate, provided a unique perspective on Ben's meteoric rise. John Ulrich described giving Ben a ride when he first turned pro. Jim Allen of Dunlop Tire discussed working with Ben throughout his distinguished AMA career. *Roadracing World's* David Swarts, the first journalist to cover Ben, shared his experiences. Tom Houseworth took on the challenge of working with a young kid, and together he and Ben became world-beaters. Brian J. Nelson, Tom Riles, Henny Ray Abrams, Andrew Wheeler, and Alan Sessarego searched their archives and provided dozens of spectacular photographs. Abrams also deserves special thanks for assisting in this project as the deadline approached. I also thank Cook Neilson and Phil Schilling of the late, great *Cycle* magazine for originally sparking my interest in motorcycles as a junior high student. As the book took shape, David Bull and his staff did a wonderful job editing and creating a beautiful finished product. And, finally, I thank my awesome wife, Jackie. Being married to a motorsports journalist is not an easy life.